W9-BFJ-893

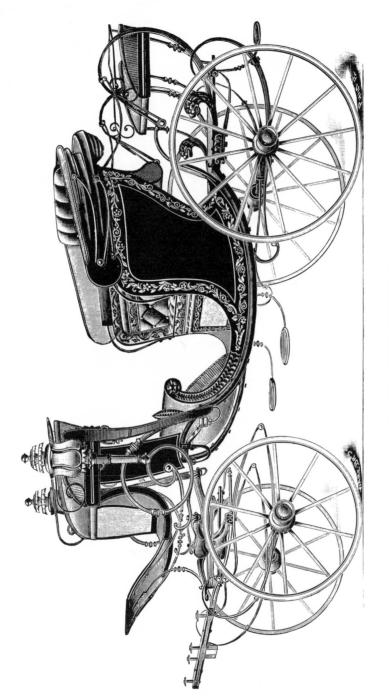

GRAND DUKE VICTORIA

(see description on page iv.)

American Carriages, Sleighs, Sulkies and Carts

168 Illustrations from Victorian Sources

Edited by

Don H. Berkebile

Associate Curator, Division of Transportation,
The Smithsonian Institution

Dover Publications, Inc.

New York

GRAND DUKE VICTORIA. (Frontispiece) This outstanding example of an elegant carriage was built by James Cunningham, Son & Co. of Rochester, N.Y., and was exhibited at the Columbian Exposition. Obsolete features such as the C-springs and the sword case on the rear were obviously for snob appeal. The rumble seat and the fine carvings are other features not often seen on a victoria. Ultramarine blue main panels and sword case. Black carved moldings striped with fine yellow. Other moldings black. Blue front carvings touched up with black. Underside of footboard blue striped with black. Yellow carriage with two pale blue stripes. Drab cloth trimming. Bedford cord driving seat. Wheels 37″ and 47″. *The Carriage Monthly*, vol. 29, Oct. 1893, pl. 47.

Copyright © 1977 by Dover Publications, Inc.
All rights reserved under Pan American and International Copyright Conventions.

Published in Canada by General Publishing Company, Ltd., 30 Lesmill Road, Don Mills, Toronto, Ontario.
Published in the United Kingdom by Constable and Company, Ltd., 10 Orange Street, London WC2H 7EG.

American Carriages, Sleighs, Sulkies and Carts: 168 Illustrations from Victorian Sources is a new work, first published by Dover Publications, Inc., in 1977.

DOVER *Pictorial Archive* SERIES

American Carriages, Sleighs, Sulkies and Carts: 168 Illustrations from Victorian Sources belongs to the Dover Pictorial Archive Series. Up to ten illustrations may be used on any one project or in any single publication free and without special permission. Wherever possible, include a credit line indicating the title of this book, author and publisher. Please address the publisher for permission to make more extensive use of illustrations in this book than that authorized above.
The reproduction of this book in whole is prohibited.

International Standard Book Number: 0-486-23328-6
Library of Congress Catalog Card Number: 76-17222

Manufactured in the United States of America
Dover Publications, Inc.
180 Varick Street
New York, N.Y. 10014

The modern American generally assumes that his ancestors used the carriage almost as freely as he uses his automobile. As he gains an awareness of the cost of acquiring and maintaining a horse and carriage, of the state of early roads and of the general lack of any need for personal transportation, he realizes that the carriage was not a common possession in eighteenth- and nineteenth-century America.

Throughout the greater part of the horse-drawn era, a carriage was the hand-fashioned product of highly skilled craftsmen such as woodworkers, wheelwrights, blacksmiths, trimmers, leather workers and painters. The number of hours these mechanics put into the construction of a vehicle prevented the average citizen from entertaining any thought of carriage ownership. Thus, those few carriages which existed in the seventeenth century, and through the first half of the eighteenth, were owned almost exclusively by persons of high office, highly successful merchants and plantation owners. While there is evidence that coaches and chariots—four-wheel vehicles—saw limited use in America during the last quarter of the seventeenth century, there is no evidence of the use of chaises and related two-wheelers until the early eighteenth century.

While an occasional reference to the use of carriages can be found during the first half of the eighteenth century, it was not until about mid-century that there was any appreciable employment of them, yet even then possession was not widespread. The number of carriages in Philadelphia in 1761, for example, was said to be 39, and in Boston in 1768 there were but 22. These figures increased to 827 in Philadelphia in 1794, and 145 in Boston in 1798. Most of these vehicles were two-wheelers. In rural areas, the cart and wagon served as both passenger and freight vehicles. In winter, in urban as well as in rural areas, sleighs were in frequent use, for, lacking such costly features as wheels, axles, fifth wheels and suspension, they cost much less. For this reason, winter was often a favorite time for travel within localities and young couples traveled by sleigh to nearby places of entertainment or to visit friends.

Following the Revolution the new nation began to show greater interest in its transportation system, and improved roads became evident. Some were operated by turnpike companies; others were financed by the federal or local governments, or by lotteries. After the turn of the nineteenth century there was also a gradual trend away from the construction of heavier carriages as improved methods of suspension such as the elliptic spring brought about marked changes in carriage design. At the same time, prosperity became more general so that greater means and additional leisure created an increasing desire for carriage ownership.

The era of the cheap carriage was still far in the future, however, for improvements in the method of building carriages occurred slowly. The only changes which began to take place in the early part of the nineteenth century were slight—occasional instances of standardized parts manufacture, whereby such items as springs, wheels and axles were purchased by carriage builders from shops specializing in the production of one or several items. Also, from patent records come indications of improvements in tools and machinery for producing certain parts. Progress in both areas was slow and of small significance during the first half of the century.

Many of the artisans who built the early carriages

in America were immigrants who had learned their skills in Europe, notably England; others were native Americans who had learned the trade from immigrant craftsmen. This, plus the fact that centuries of European tradition had developed a number of satisfactory carriage styles, dictated that the carriages first used here should follow English and Continental lines. After 1800, and especially between 1830 and 1860, several distinctive American carriage types began to develop and, at the same time, American designers made significant modifications in existing European styles.

The emergence of trade literature in the 1850s evidences the growth of the carriage industry. In 1853 C. W. Saladee of Columbus, Ohio, introduced his *Coach-makers' Guide*, which was succeeded by *The American Coach-makers' Illustrated Monthly Magazine* in 1855. In 1858 came Ezra Stratton's *New York Coach-maker's Magazine*, which in 1871 was absorbed into *The Hub*, soon to become one of America's two leading carriage journals. The other leader started in 1865 under the title of the *Coach-maker's International Journal*, acquiring the better-known title of *The Carriage Monthly* in 1873. Trade catalogs also began to be issued by some of the leading carriage builders in the 60s, so that from this time onward we have a complete and accurate record of the many styles of carriages that were in use. It is largely from this record that the illustrations in this volume have been chosen.

During the last quarter of the century, the carriage industry emerged from the handcraft stage as the effects of the American industrial revolution finally overtook the trade. Even as the 70s began, machinery was in only limited use (mainly for sawing) and carriage builders were of the general opinion that machinery could not be effectively employed in any but the largest factories. The first widespread use of mass-production techniques began in several Cincinnati carriage shops during the mid 70s. Specialized machines processed the many wood parts of a carriage; malleable iron castings minimized the work of the smith shop by eliminat-

ing many hours of forge work. These malleable castings, along with numerous other parts, were not made in the carriage shops, but were produced by the growing numbers of specialty parts manufacturers. Thus, as gear and body irons, axles, wheels, springs, lamps, dashes, whip sockets, top fittings and shafts and other bentwood parts were purchased, the carriage building became more of an assembler and finisher.

The result was the cheap carriage, which opened up a new market in rural America. In an earlier day, the farmer gave little thought to owning a carriage; it was a luxury he could seldom afford. Indeed, he had little need for a carriage, for his rude farm wagon could, if necessary, furnish transportation for his family. As the price of a buggy began to decline, falling into the "three for a hundred" range by 1900, the farmer saw for the first time that he could enjoy the comfort of a vehicle equipped with springs. When his first buggy wore out, he bought another, or often decided he could afford something like a surrey or a carriage even more costly.

The increasing market, in turn, led to the development of more sophisticated machinery. Improvements in drop forges resulted in some substitution of drop forgings for malleable iron castings, thus upgrading the quality of the work. By 1900 an ordinary buggy could be purchased, exclusive of horse and harness, for just slightly more than a tradesman's monthly wages, while a comparable vehicle in the 1860s would have cost him nearly seven months' wages ($125–$150). The methods by which these economy carriages were produced were soon copied by the automobile industry. It learned that mass production was necessary to produce the quantity of goods for the largest and most lucrative market—the working classes. The 1900 census figures show that 907,483 pleasure carriages were built in that year, up 8 percent over the 1890 figure. In addition, 118,221 sleighs were built, up 36 percent over 1890.

In spite of the increasing popularity of the carriage, however, there was never a significant trend toward carriage ownership among the urban working classes. The cost of the carriage was not always the drawback, for added to this was the cost of purchasing and maintaining a horse with harness, and the problem of housing the animal and vehicle. The need for a private carriage was not great, for the larger cities had adequate public transportation systems, and long working hours cut short the time allowed for pleasure and recreation. When the occasional need did arise, the livery stable could take care of it. One automotive pioneer, Hiram P. Maxim, felt that the auto was the successor to the bicycle rather than to the carriage, for in his view it was the cycle and not the carriage that had taught Americans the value and desirability of individual transportation, independent of the fixed schedules of public transportation. The 1890s were, after all, the decade of the safety bicycle, and during the last half of this same period the interest in automobiles increased rapidly, while similar efforts toward mechanical propulsion in earlier decades had attracted little serious interest. Perhaps Maxim's assessment was not groundless.

The carriages represented in this book have been arranged according to structure in the following manner: two-wheel vehicles (plates 1–26); light four-wheel vehicles (plates 27–70); four-wheel vehicles, owner-driven (plates 71–102); four-wheel vehicles, coachman-driven (plates 103–142); four-in-hand vehicles (plates 143–145); sleighs (plates 146–161). There is also a section showing detailed trimming patterns for several types of popular vehicles (plates 162–167).

Since this collection of illustrations can be of assistance to model builders, carriage restorers and artists, the captions frequently include notes on finish and trimmings, along with a few basic dimensions to denote scale. Too often the earlier journals fail to include this information, so it should be pointed out that during the 1850s and 60s a greater variety of colors was more commonly seen. While black undoubtedly led the array, other colors appear to have exceeded it collectively. Dark and medium browns were most popular, while various reds, some approaching purple, were frequently used on many of the heavier carriages. The darker blues were also widely seen. The darker greens were only beginning to come into use, though not nearly with the frequency which they later enjoyed. The body and running gear of a carriage were sometimes painted the same color; perhaps as often they were different colors. Panels and moldings often differed in color. The belt-rail was sometimes black, like the moldings, and an occasional special panel was at times some bright color. Creams and yellows were generally reserved for running gears.

An attractive feature of the carriages of the 50s and 60s was their striping. Some bodies were not striped; some had gold or some other color on the moldings. On the gears, however, the striping was more evident, for it was often of two or even three colors. A heavy stripe was first applied, over which finer stripes of one or more colors were laid. These finer stripes variously centered on, edged, or were perhaps set in slightly from the edges of the broad stripes. Popular striping colors, harmonious with the background, were black, red, white, blue, gold, brown, yellow, purple, orange and green.

The plates in this book are generally accurate scale drawings, yet some carriage draftsmen, in order to simplify their drawings, decreased the number of spokes in the wheels. Front wheels usually had 14 spokes, with 16 in the rear, though two spokes less per wheel would be suitable if the wheels were of less than the usual diameters. If front and rear wheels were nearly the same size, they might have the same number of spokes.

THE PRINCIPAL PARTS OF A CARRIAGE

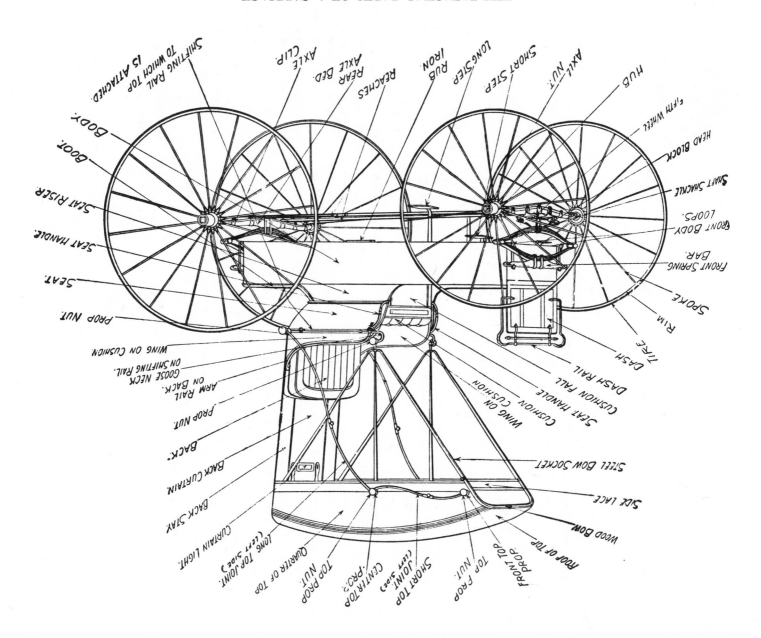

1. CURRICLE. An early style of carriage that saw only the most limited use by the end of the 19th century, the curricle was equipped with a single pole and was drawn by two horses abreast. Black body. Olive green carriage striped black. Green cloth trimming. Wheels 50″. *The Hub*, vol. 37, July 1895, pl. 166.

2. CHAISE. One of the most popular vehicles in both England and America during the 18th and early 19th centuries was the chaise, a name for any two-wheel, one-horse vehicle. This rare piece in the Smithsonian Institution was built in Massachusetts in the 1770s. The driver's seat is an unusual feature, and qualifies this carriage as a "calash."

3. CHAISE. Suspended on leather thoroughbraces and wooden cantilever springs, vehicles of this type were often known as New England or Boston chaises. They were com- monly called "shays" by Americans. This one, from the Smithsonian Institution, dates from about 1830.

4. CHAISE. By 1862 the once-popular vehicle was nearly obsolete. A few manufacturers, however, still offered them. Lawrence, Bradley & Pardee, of New Haven, Conn., listed this one in their 1862 catalog.

5. CABRIOLET. The cabriolet was first developed in Italy and France in the late 17th century as a two-wheeler. This 1860 model in the English style evolved from it. Used to a limited extent in America, it had the front top-joints mounted inside, so that the first top-bow could be readily pushed back to allow easier egress. Wheels 52″. *The New York Coachmaker's Magazine,* vol. 2, Feb. 1860, pl. 31.

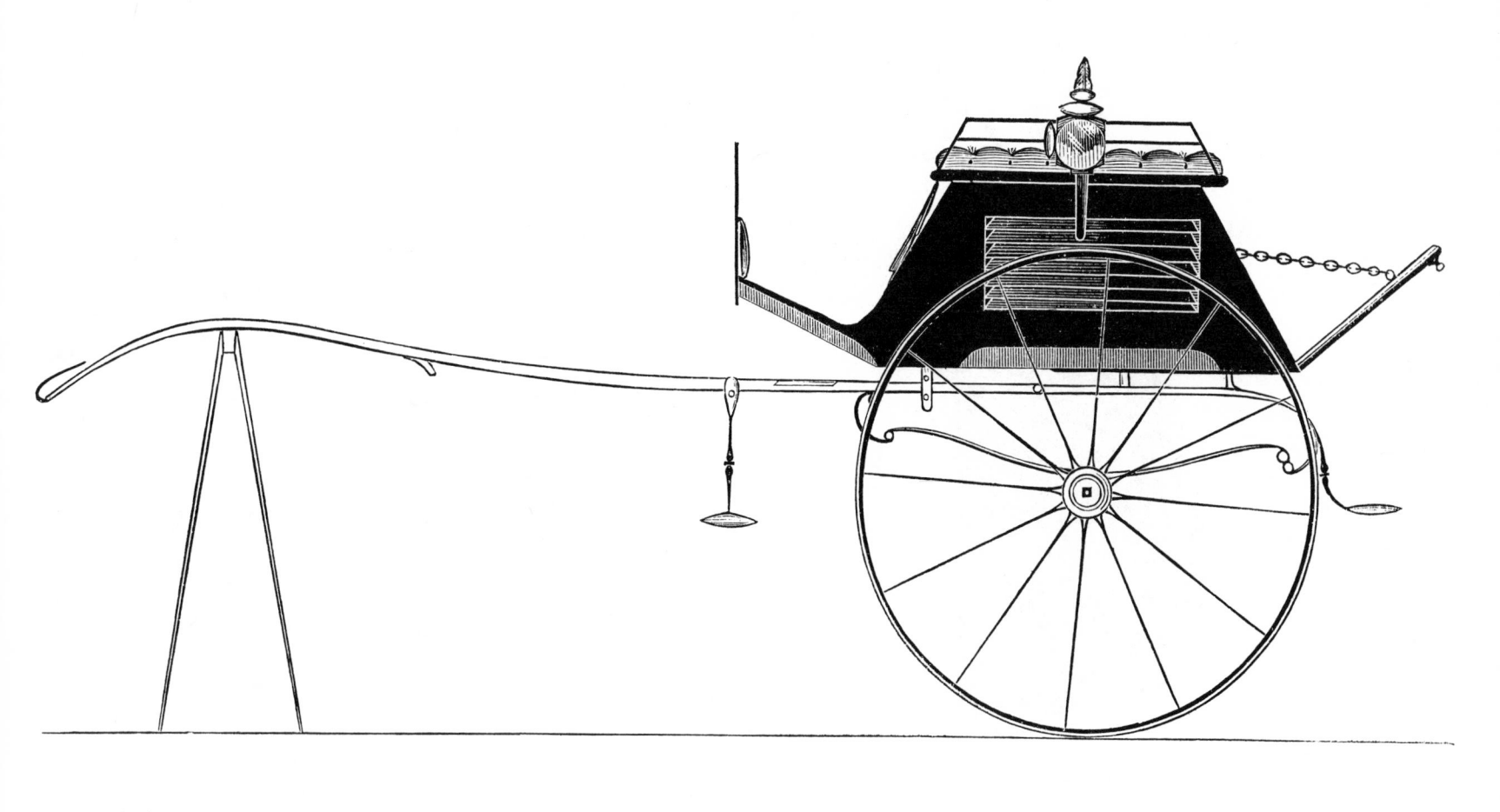

6. DOG CART. The dog cart developed from the 18th-century English shooting gig. While intended as a sporting vehicle, it attained great popularity as a general-purpose passenger vehicle. When it was used as a hunting cart, the dogs were carried in the slat-ventilated box under the seats, while one or two grooms or additional passengers faced toward the rear with their feet resting on the lowered end-gate. Frequently drawn by a single horse, the dog cart could be driven tandem, using the hook shown on the end of the shaft. Wheels 53″. *The New York Coach-maker's Magazine,* vol. 10, Oct. 1868, pl. 18.

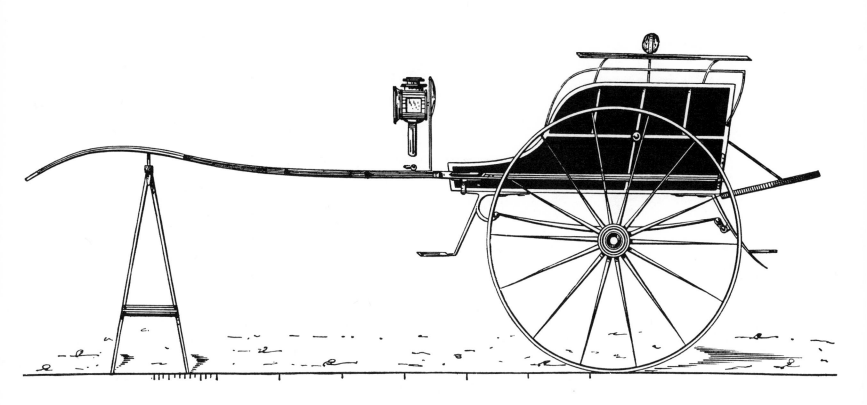

7. DOG CART. This New York designed dog cart looks a little less top heavy. The rear ends of the shafts could be raised or lowered, according to the load, to help balance the body. Black body striped with vermilion. Lake carriage striped with vermilion. Bedford cord trimming. Wheels 48″. *The Hub*, vol. 24, Oct. 1882, pl. 73.

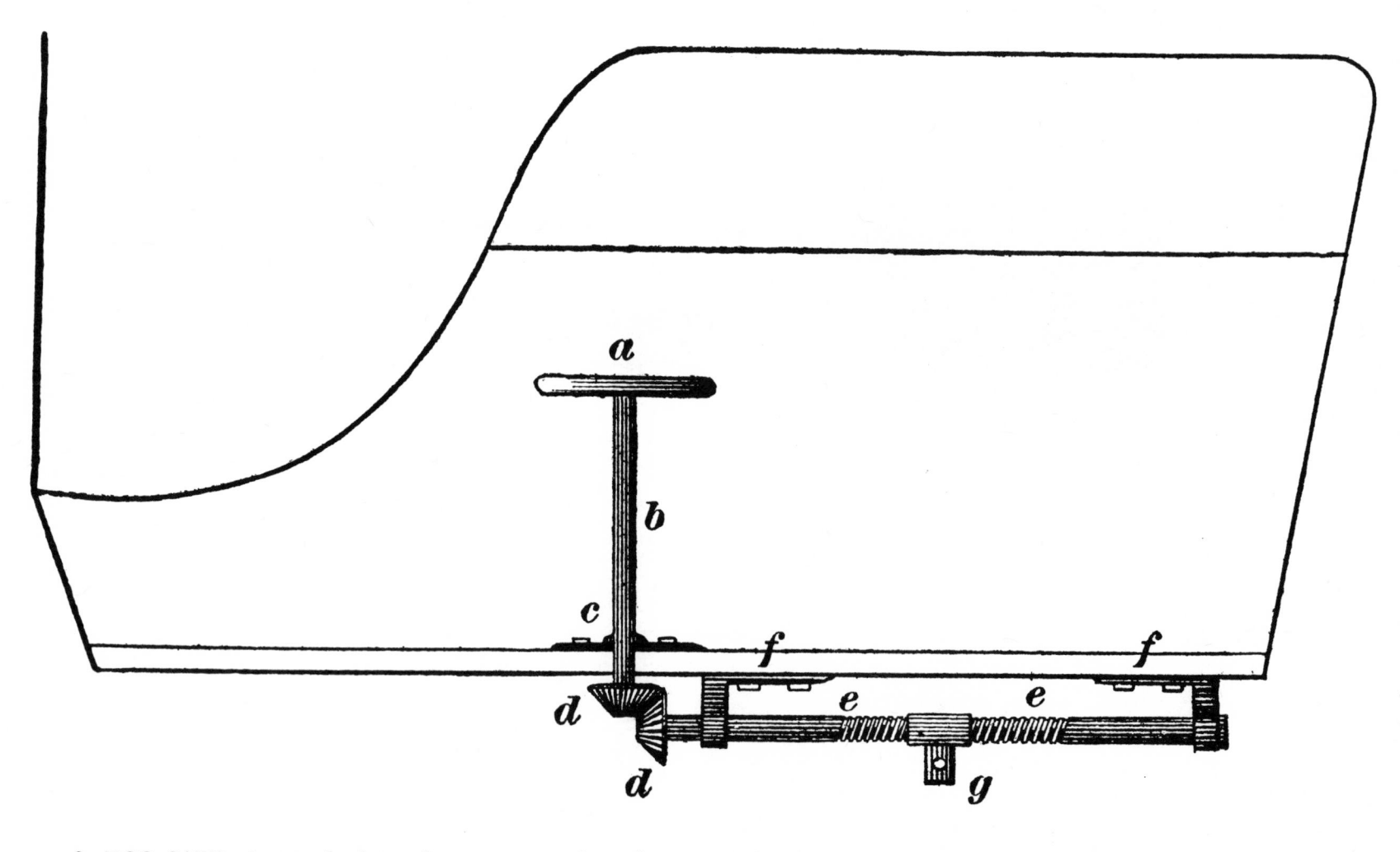

8. DOG CART. A two-wheeler with two seats, such as the dog cart, cannot balance properly if there is not a full load. Many devices, such as the mechanism shown here, were used to adjust the body, forward or backward, to accommodate any given load. Wheels 58″. Track 56″. Body 35″ wide at the bottom. *The Hub,* vol. 32, Aug. 1890, p. 358.

9. WHITECHAPEL CART. One of the many designs borrowed from English carriage builders was the Whitechapel cart, a variety of dog cart which began to find some favor in the United States in the late 1860s. The body styling of the dog cart also influenced development of the surrey. Dark green body with black moldings. Light vermilion or yellow carriage with a ½″ black stripe. Bedford cord or dark green cloth trimming. Wheels 54″. Track 58″. *The Hub,* vol. 23, Sept. 1881, pl. 60.

10. TANDEM CART. Drawn, as the name indicates, by two horses harnessed in tandem, this was a sporting vehicle that tested one's skill as a driver. Essentially it was a dog cart, featuring high suspension. Imitation cane work, cream. Vermilion blinds and bracket panel. Black moldings. Vermilion carriage with two black stripes. Light Bedford cord trimming. *The Hub*, vol. 26, Feb. 1885, p. 774.

11. TANDEM CART. This plate gives a better view of the driving seat and a glimpse of part of the mechanical device that allowed the body to be shifted to better distribute the weight, according to whether there were two, three, or four passengers. Some used a large screw at the rear; others a hand screw that was operated from the driving seat. Deep green panels with black moldings, surrounded by slats and moldings of Indian red. Area between moldings on front brackets, deep green. Indian red seat riser. Deep green carriage with two stripes of Indian red. Green cloth trimming. Wheels 46″. Width at seat bottom, 36″. *The Carriage Monthly*, vol. 34, Aug. 1898, pl. 21.

12. GOVERNESS CART. A relatively late development in horse-drawn vehicles was the governess cart, an English design that gained some popularity in the United States. With two seats along the sides like a wagonette, and a door in the rear, it was commonly used as a children's cart. This one has a paneled body, but many had bodies of wickerwork. Black body. Deep olive green seat panels. Yellow canework. Olive green carriage striped black. Light whipcord trimming. Wheels 42″. Track 54″. Body 46″ wide at the top. *The Hub*, vol. 44, Jan. 1903, pl. 589.

13. GOVERNESS CART. This photo of a wickerwork governess cart was taken about 1900. Note the cranked (or drop-center) axle, which permitted lower suspension of the body. (Photo from Smithsonian Institution.)

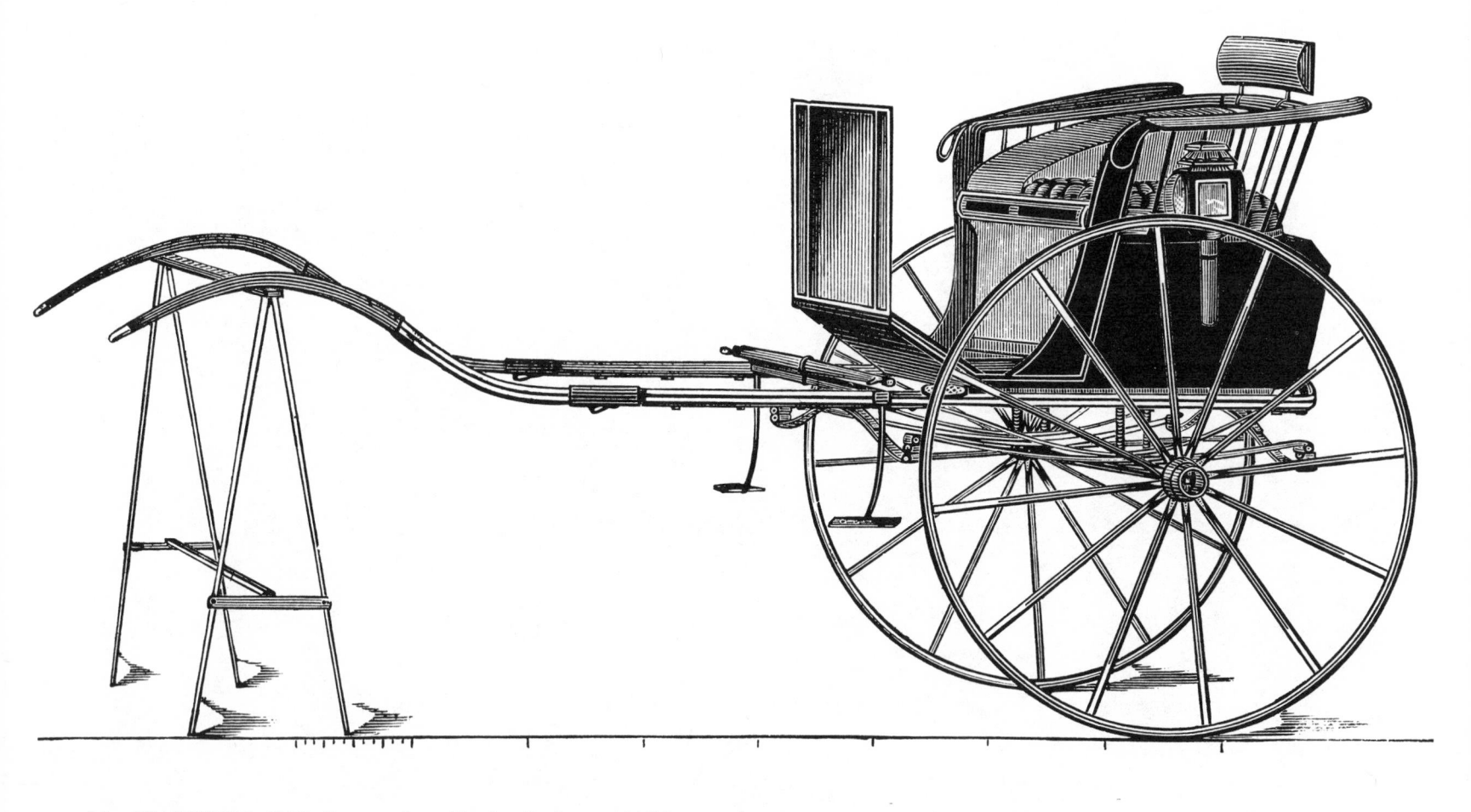

14. STANHOPE GIG. Invented in England about 1815 by Fitzroy Stanhope, the stanhope gig was characterized both by its body, which lent its pillar to many other carriages, and by its suspension on two side springs and two cross springs. It was usually drawn by one horse, although it could also be driven with two in tandem. Though most popular during its earlier history, it continued in use throughout the horse-drawn era. A gentleman's vehicle, it was frequently seen at horse shows. Black body with dark green pillars. Dark green carriage striped pearl. Dark green cloth trimmings. Wheels 52″. Body 38″ wide. *The Hub,* vol. 24, Mar. 1883, pl. 112.

15. STANHOPE GIG. Black body and seat panels. Lake moldings striped with a fine line of vermilion. Lake carriage striped with one broad line and two fine lines of vermilion. Maroon cloth trimming. *The Carriage Monthly*, vol. 38, Sept. 1902, pl. 631.

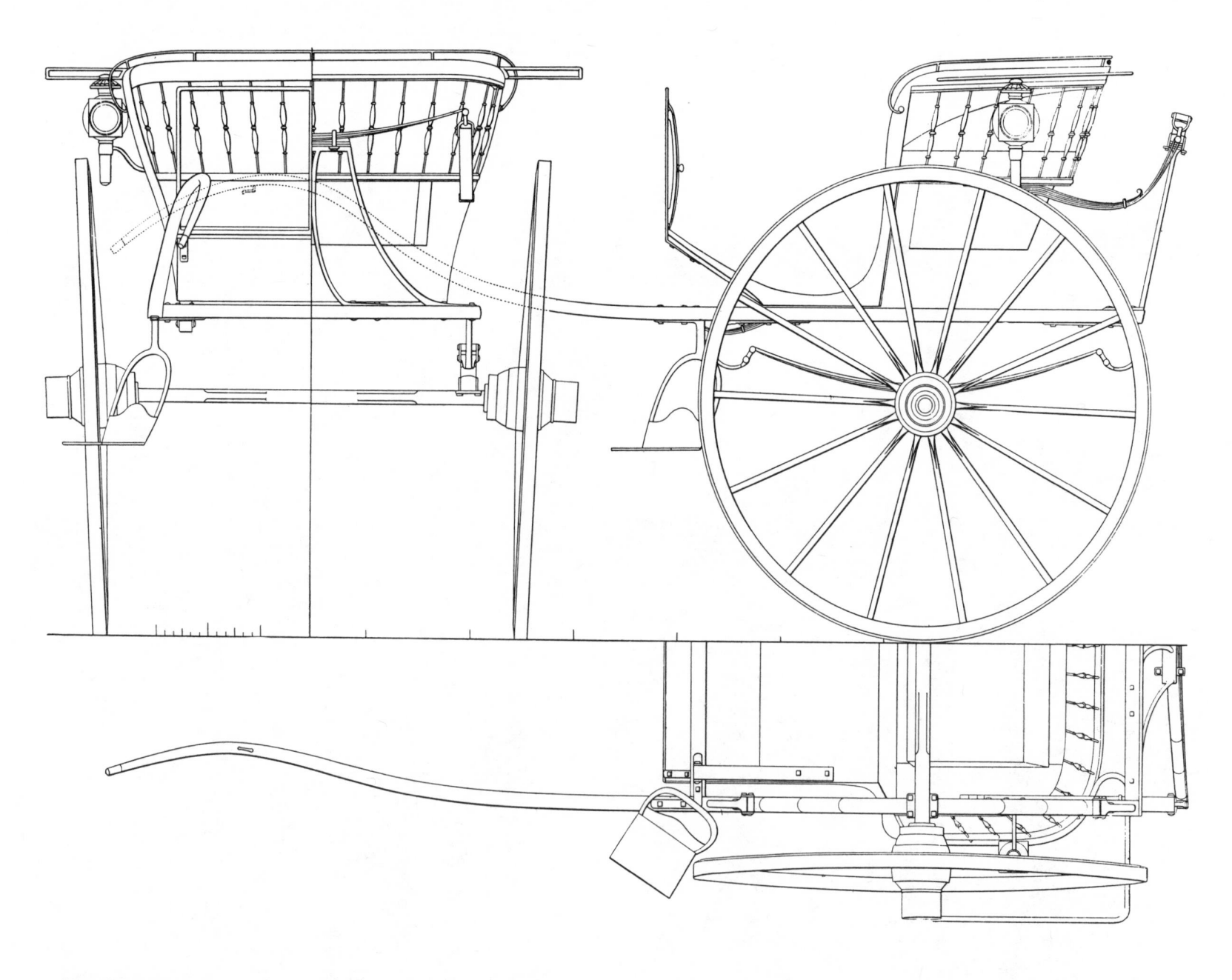

16. TILBURY. A companion to the stanhope gig was the tilbury, also designed in about 1815 by Fitzroy Stanhope. A most fashionable gentleman's vehicle, it was characterized by 7-spring suspension, though later other methods were some-times employed. After initial popularity, it lost favor, but re-gained it by the end of the century. Black body with carmine seat spindles. Carmine carriage striped black. Buff corduroy trimming. *The Hub*, vol. 36, June 1894, p. 184.

17. HANSOM CAB. Named after English architect Joseph A. Hansom, who patented the original design in 1834, this vehicle was greatly improved in later years. After several unsuccessful attempts to introduce it in the United States, it gained some acceptance late in the century, particularly in New York City, where, as in London, it was used mainly as a public cab. Lower quarters and back panels of body dark green. Upper quarters of body, back panels, driver's seat and moldings black striped with two fine lines of light green. Dark green carriage with broad vermilion stripe and two fine lines of light green. Blue cloth trimming. Wheels 56″. Body 48¼″ wide. *The Hub*, vol. 27, Feb. 1886, pl. 83.

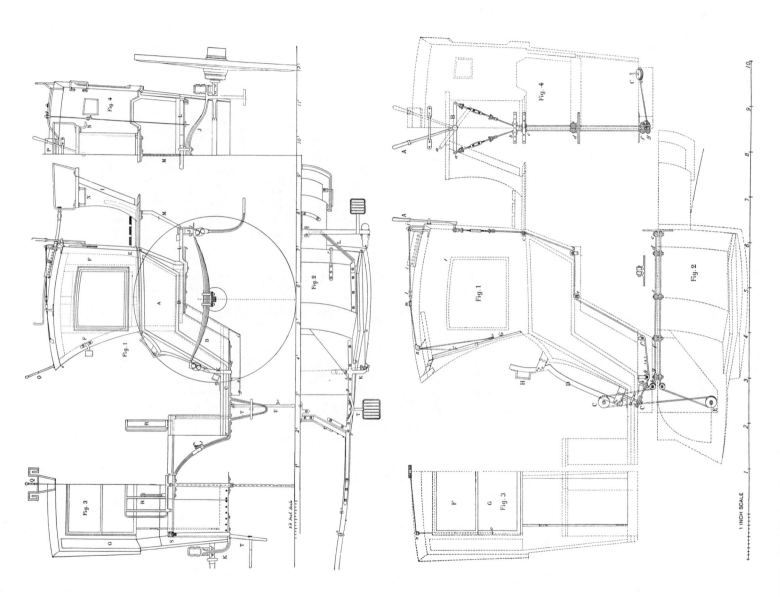

18. HANSOM CAB. These drawings show the arrangements by which the doors and front window of a Hansom cab could be opened and closed from the driver's seat in the rear. The ironwork on the front of the roof (labeled Q in figs. 1 and 3 of the top drawing) supported the lines leading to the horse. *The Carriage Monthly,* vol. 35, July 1899, pp. 107, 109.

19. PRIVATE HANSOM. The private Hansom was intended for business purposes. The rear driver's seat, doors and front windows of the public cab model were dispensed with to decrease weight. Deep green body with black upper panels and rockers. Yellow carriage with two ¼" black stripes. Green cloth trimming. Wheels 51". *The Carriage Monthly*, vol. 23, Dec. 1887, pl. 74.

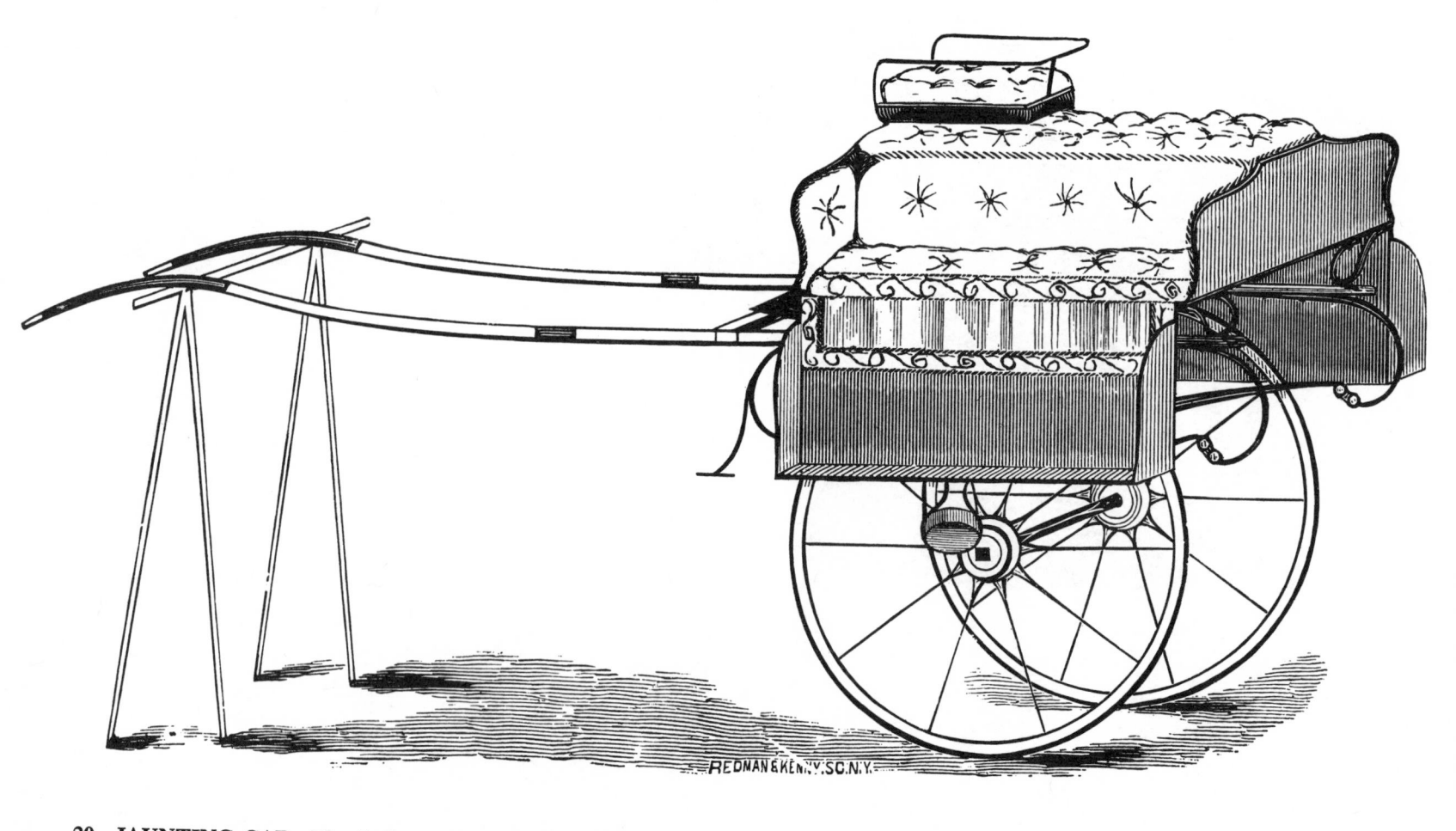

20. JAUNTING CAR. The Irish jaunting car was little used in the United States. Persons unaccustomed to riding over the wheels on the longitudinal seats were likely to be thrown off if the vehicle rounded curves too rapidly. *Carriage Drafts selected from the New York Coach-maker's Magazine and The Hub*. New York, 1873, pl. 294.

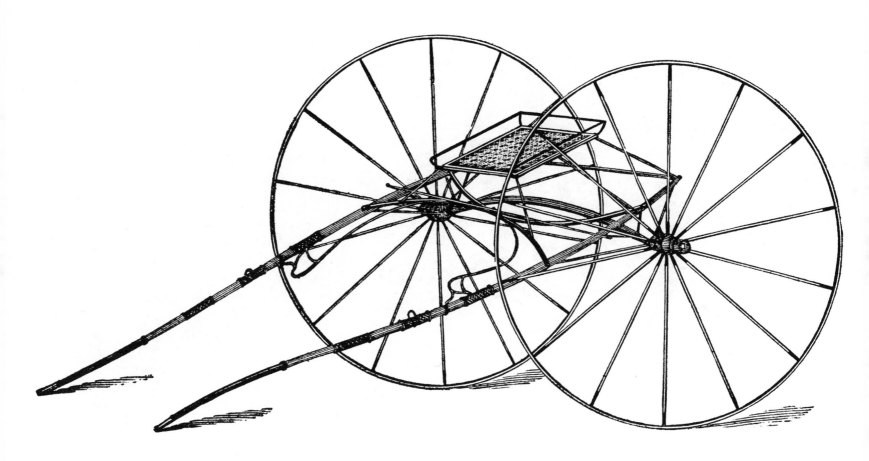

21. SULKY. The term "sulky" was applied in mid-18th-century England to any vehicle designed for a single passenger. Later, in America, it was applied to chaises and chairs that could carry only one. By the early 19th century the sulky was a skeleton two-wheeler like this one, used on the race track. Carmine with black stripes and gold mountings. Wheels 56". *The Carriage Monthly*, vol. 15, June 1879, pl. 16.

22. SPLIT-SHAFT SULKY. Phineas Jones & Co., of Newark, N.J., the noted wheel makers, built this model. Weighing about 45 pounds, it featured shafts made of two pieces, glued together at the ends, but separated in the center. This was a safety feature, for if one half of the shaft broke, the other half would not necessarily follow. Carmine with black stripes. Wheels 55″. *The Hub*, vol. 27, Dec. 1885, color pl. LXVI.

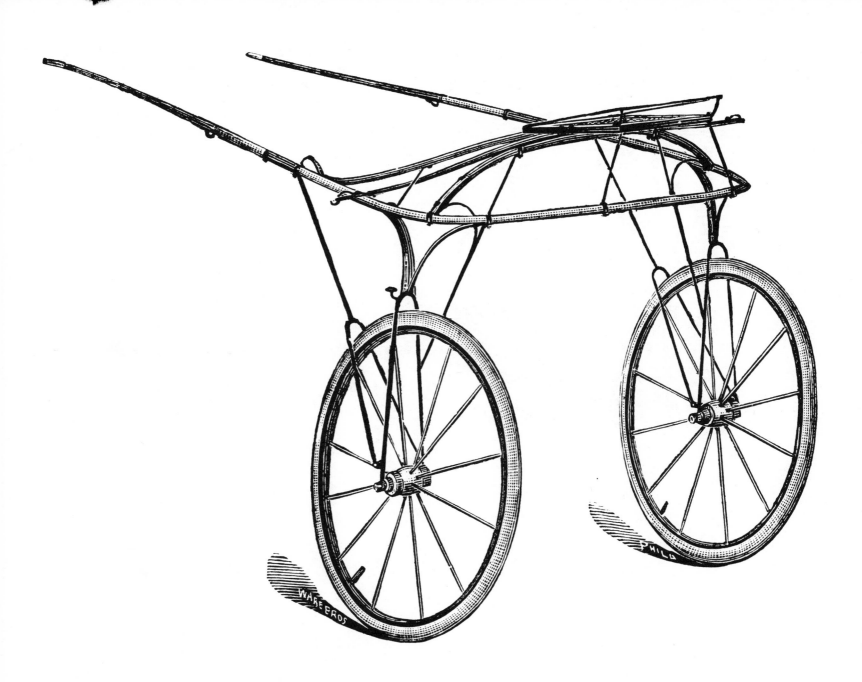

23. SULKY. The sulky was the first horse-drawn vehicle to see widespread use of the pneumatic tire, beginning in 1892. This gave rise to the name "bicycle sulky." While this one, like some bicycles, has wooden spoke wheels, many used the wire spokes of the more common bicycle wheel. Carmine or orange-yellow with two black stripes. Silver mountings. *The Carriage Monthly,* vol. 29, Aug. 1893, pl. 36.

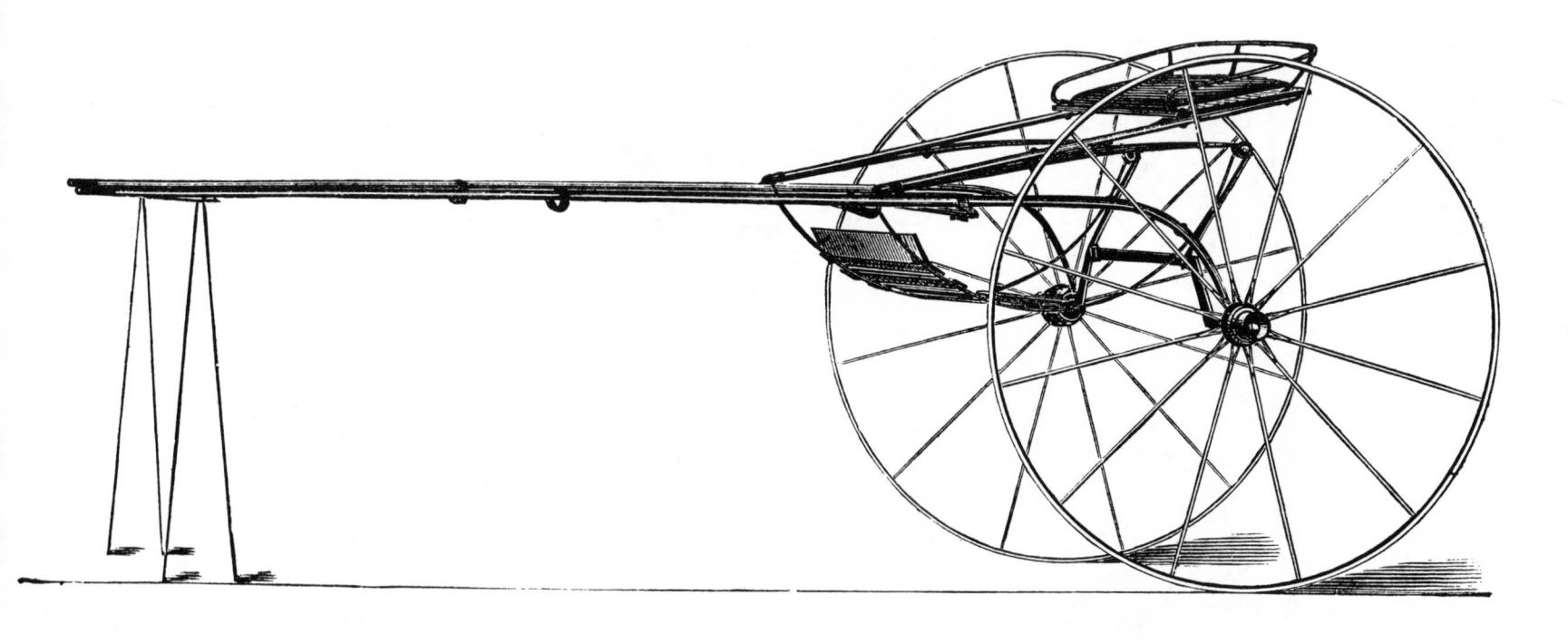

24. ROAD CART. The term was supposedly introduced about 1881; the vehicle was previously known as a sulky. It was intended for use on the road rather than on the track. Some had seating for two. Many rural mail carriers found them convenient for their work. By 1900 a road cart could be purchased for $8 to $15. Dark green with black mountings. Wheels 48″. *The Carriage Monthly*, vol. 8, Oct. 1882, pl. 55.

25. ROAD CART. For those interested in increased comfort and better appearance, phaeton-body road carts were also available, complete with falling top. Black body. Red carriage striped black. Black leather trimmings. Wheels 52″. Catalog of the Studebaker Bros. Mfg. Co., South Bend, Ind., Dec. 1903.

26. PONY CART. Light, attractive pony carts, popular with ladies and children, were furnished with wheels of varying sizes to agree with the size of pony used. Bodies were infrequently black, while the carriage parts were optionally black, Brewster green, pea green, carmine, red, yellow or blue. The trimming could be whipcord, Bedford cord, figured plush, green broadcloth or leather. In the early 1900s, a pony cart cost from $25 to $35. (Photo from Smithsonian Institution.)

THE HUB.N.Y.

27. BEACH WAGON. Intended for four or more passengers, this type of vehicle came in a great variety of styles. Some builders would have called this one a depot wagon or a carryall, but Quimby & Co., of Newark, N.J. called it a beach wagon. As its name suggests, it was intended as a recreational or outing vehicle. Lower body panels, black. Space between moldings, dark green. Dark green carriage with two fine stripes of light green. Green leather trimming with green cloth head lining. Wheels 40″ and 48″. Body 40½″ wide. *The Hub,* vol. 25, Feb. 1884, pl. 88.

28. BEACH WAGON. This open model was built by the Connor Carriage Co., of Amesbury, Mass. Some builders would have called this a cabriolet; others a park phaeton. *The Hub,* vol. 40, Sept. 1898, p. 442.

29. BEACH WAGON. A model featuring an unusual vis-à-vis arrangement. Each seat could accommodate three persons. Black body and seats. Toeboard and latticework under the rear seats yellow. Red carriage with black iron parts. Russet leather trimming. Wheels 35″ and 45″. Body 39″ wide. Seat 48″ wide. *The Hub,* vol. 41, Oct. 1899, pl. 444.

30. BUCKBOARD. A true buckboard had one or several tough, flexible boards serving both as a floor and the sole means of suspension. Features characteristic of this type are the wooden dash and, on many better models, a natural finish.

Body and carriage with natural wood finish. Green cloth trimmings. Wheels 42″ and 46″. *The Carriage Monthly*, vol. 26, July 1890, pl. 31.

31. BUCKBOARD. Buckboards were also built with several seats, as shown by this Studebaker style made for use in Yellowstone Park. Though the body is still unsprung, the ride is improved by elliptic springs under the seats. Wheels 42″ and 50″. *The Hub,* vol. 29, May 1887, pl. 13.

32. BUCKBOARD. Later buckboards often had spring suspension, such as this model with Brewster and torsion end springs. Dark green body. Carmine carriage. Leather trimmings. Wheels 40″ and 44″. Catalog of the Studebaker Bros. Mfg. Co., South Bend, Ind., Dec. 1903.

33. BIKE WAGON. One of the last developments of the carriage era was this vehicle, using wire wheels, pneumatic or solid rubber tires, ball- or roller-bearing hubs and often tubular steel running gears. *The Hub*, vol. 41, Oct. 1899, p. 298.

34. COAL-BOX BUGGY. Introduced in about 1862, this buggy's resemblance to a coal box gave it its name. It enjoyed an immense popularity for several decades. As shown in this plate, the top of a carriage of this type was often lowered but not completely folded, because tops wore badly along the creases. Body and carriage either black striped gold, or lake striped red. Blue cloth trimming. Wheels 47″ and 52″. *The New York Coach-maker's Magazine*, vol. 5, July 1863, pl. 16.

35. COAL-BOX BUGGY. The coal-box buggy caught on quickly; by 1866 it was the most fashionable buggy in New York City. Black body and carriage. Carriage with broad stripes of either dark blue or red. Dark blue cloth trimming. Wheels 45″ and 48″. *The New York Coach-maker's Magazine*, vol. 8, Dec. 1866, pl. 28.

36. COAL-BOX BUGGY. A variant of the coal-box buggy in the southern states often had a turn-out seat for a child. Black body. Dark green carriage striped vermilion. Dark green cloth trimming. Wheels 44″ and 46″. *The Carriage Monthly,* vol. 18, June 1882, pl. 23.

THE HUB, N.Y.

37. COAL-BOX BUGGY. This model from Illinois had a slightly different design with a drop-front allowing easier access. Black body. Dark brown seat with a fine stripe of buff on the moldings. Dark brown carriage with two fine stripes of buff. Dark brown cloth trimming. Wheels 45″ and 48″. *The Hub,* vol. 22, Mar. 1881, pl. 130.

38. CORNING BUGGY. The deep rear portion of the body and the cut-down front are distinctive of a Corning buggy (also called a Whitechapel wagon or buggy because of its resemblance to the forerunner of the surrey). Black body. Dark green carriage striped with a lighter green. Dark green cloth trimming. Wheels 45″ and 48″. Track 52″. Body 40″ wide. *The Hub*, vol. 22, Mar. 1881, pl. 129.

39. PIANO-BOX BUGGY. Introduced around the mid-1850s, the piano-box buggy became the most popular horse-drawn vehicle in America, if not the world. It was comparable to the Model T Ford of a later era. Wheels, 48″ and 50″. *The New York Coach-maker's Magazine*, vol. 10 June 1868, pl. 4.

40. PIANO-BOX BUGGY. An ordinary model with falling top, mounted on a bike gear. Black body. Red, blue, green, or yellow carriage appropriately striped. Wheels 34″ and 36″. Catalog of H. H. Babcock Co., Watertown, N.Y. 1902.

41. JUMP-SEAT PIANO-BOX BUGGY. These were popular vehicles during the 60s and 70s, offering either two- or four-passenger capacity at will. The front seat could be "jumped" out of the way and the rear seat slid forward to give it the appearance of an ordinary buggy. Many buggies of this period were either black with a quarter-inch gold stripe, or lake striped with red. This one appears to have panels of some contrasting color. Trimmings were most often of blue cloth. Wheels 44″ and 48″. Catalog of Lawrence, Bradley and Pardee, New Haven, 1862.

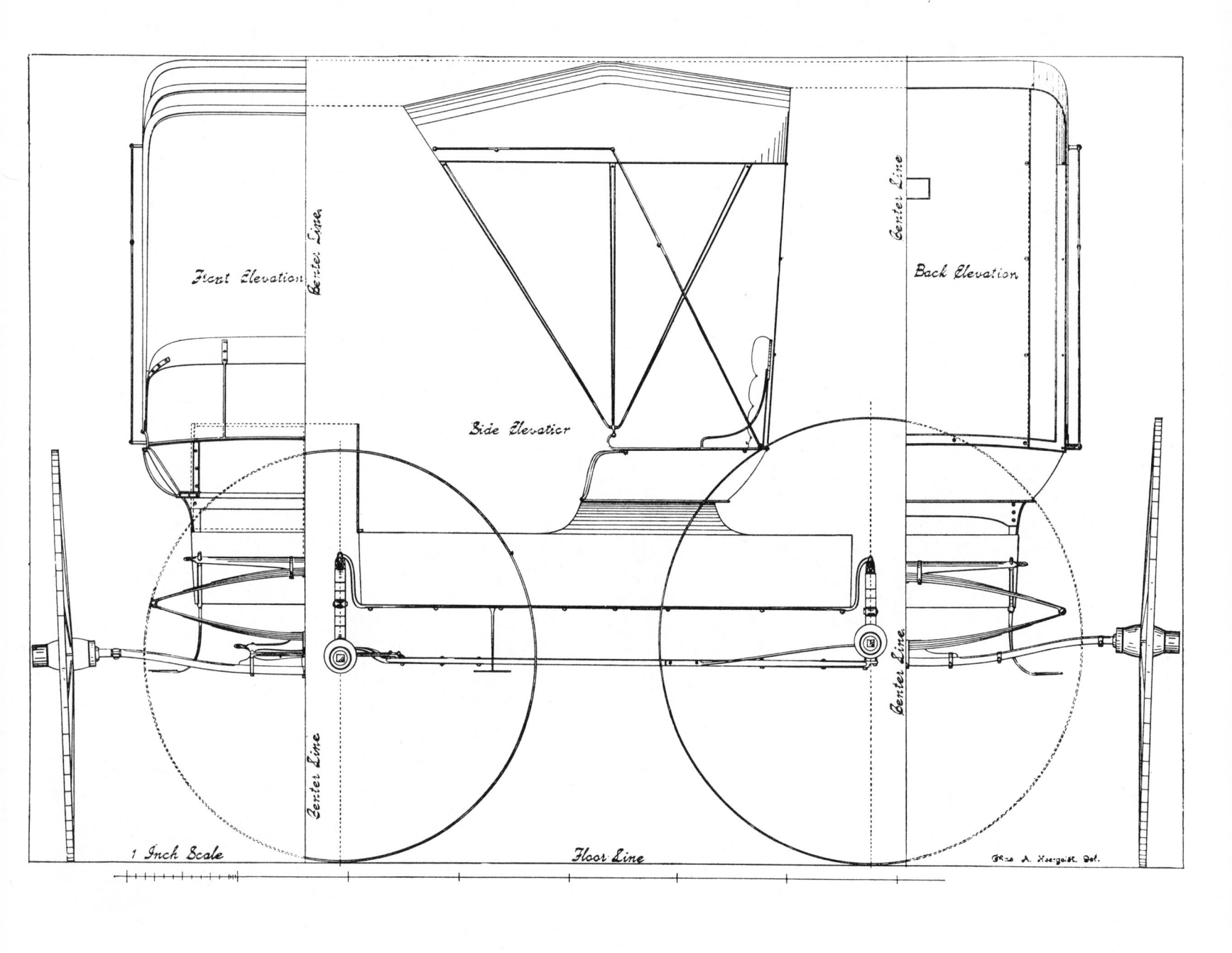

Front Elevation

Center Line

Side Elevation

Back Elevation

Center Line

Center Line

Center Line

1 Inch Scale

Floor Line

Geo. A. Heergeist. Del.

42. PIANO-BOX BUGGY. This is a most common late design, on two elliptic springs. Black body. Red or yellow carriage striped black. Green cloth trimming. Wheels 42″ and 46″. *The Carriage Monthly,* vol. 30, Dec. 1894, p. 265.

43. BREWSTER BUGGY. A piano-box, but with the Brewster name because of the manner of suspension—side bars with body attached by means of two springs running underneath. Catalog of the H. H. Babcock Co., Watertown, N.Y. 1895.

$31.85 ═══ "SOUTHERN" SPECIAL BUGGY ═══ $31.85

BUILT
FOR DEALERS AND
TRADERS TO SELL

ALSO FOR THOSE
WHO CAN AFFORD
TO INVEST ONLY
THIS AMOUNT IN A
BUGGY

ORDER
WIDE OR
NARROW
TRACK

HALF PATENT ONE PIECE STEEL AXLES.

$31.85 No matter what the price, we furnish good wheels with tires properly set. If the owner will keep the tires tight and have them reset whenever it becomes necessary, he will have reason to feel **more than satisfied** with any buggy he has bought of us. This buggy is built for those who are willing to pay dealers and our competitors more money for work that has been constructed of the cheapest "odd material" that can be collected. Do not class any of our vehicles with what our competitors offer. **These Buggies are not handled by any other Chicago firm.** We put them through the factory in quantities, building every one as described.

SEE EXTRAS BELOW, NO OTHER CHANGES

It is better value than offered heretofore by any firm for such a small sum. We **guarantee every part against defects for two years.** We urge you to invest more money in a buggy as the difference in price will be more than offset by the **longer service.**

WHEELS are Sarven patent, ⅞ inch **steel tires full bolted.** Height 38 and 42 inches, or if preferred 36 and 40, or 40 and 44, also ¾ inch tire. Wheels are made of hickory throughout.

GEAR **One piece best steel axles,** double collar, drop as illustrated, or arch if so ordered. Hickory gear woods throughout, including double reaches **ironed full length.** Rear king bolt fifth wheel. Elliptic end springs, or if so ordered Brewster side bar springs at same price. Second growth hickory spring bars.

BODY is **piano box** 23 inches wide and 54 inches long. Yellow poplar panels, heavy ash sills and concave risers (no other firm will furnish yellow poplar panel and concave risers on any buggy they sell for less than $40.00). **Corners screwed, glued and plugged.** Will not warp and twist out of shape. Can furnish Corning body if preferred. Full width seat nicely finished.

TRIMMING of both seat and back cushion is imitation leather. Color is dark green. Upholstered back cushion as illustrated. Full drop back is furnished. Half length carpet, boot, nickel seat handles, dash rail and wrench supplied, but **no storm apron.**

TOP is enamel drill throughout including side curtains. Furnished three bow regularly or four bow if so ordered. While this **top is guaranteed against defective material** we recommend that a rubber top be ordered, as it will last much longer and the extra cost is small. See extra cost under price.

PAINTING Body is painted black and nicely striped as shown. Gear Brewster green and striped. Weight crated, about 500 lbs.

NO. 3M 166

Price complete	$31.85
Extra, full rubber top	1.25
Long distance axles	1.00
Bailey body loops	1.00
Pole in place of shafts	2.00
Pole in addition to shafts	4.00

Shipped direct from factory to you.

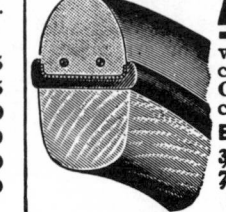

Rubber TIRES
will add more than twice their cost to the value of any vehicle. Guaranteed. They increase the comfort, appearance and service.
EXTRA IN PLACE OF STEEL TIRES.

¾-inch	$13.50
⅞-inch	14.75
1-inch	16.00

44. PIANO-BOX BUGGY. It was hard to beat the prices of the Cash Buyers' Union, which offered economy piano-boxes like this for $31.85, or occasionally less. The average model cost about $45. By the turn of the century bodies were almost always black, but the carriage part could be black, dark green, yellow, red, carmine or maroon. The common green trimming was so dark that it was almost black. Catalog of the Cash Buyers' Union, Chicago, Ill. 1903.

45. PIANO-BOX BUGGY. Drawn by a horse wearing a breast-collar harness, this model dates from the 1900s. The top has been dropped, but not completely folded, to avoid excessive wear. (Photo from Smithsonian Institution.)

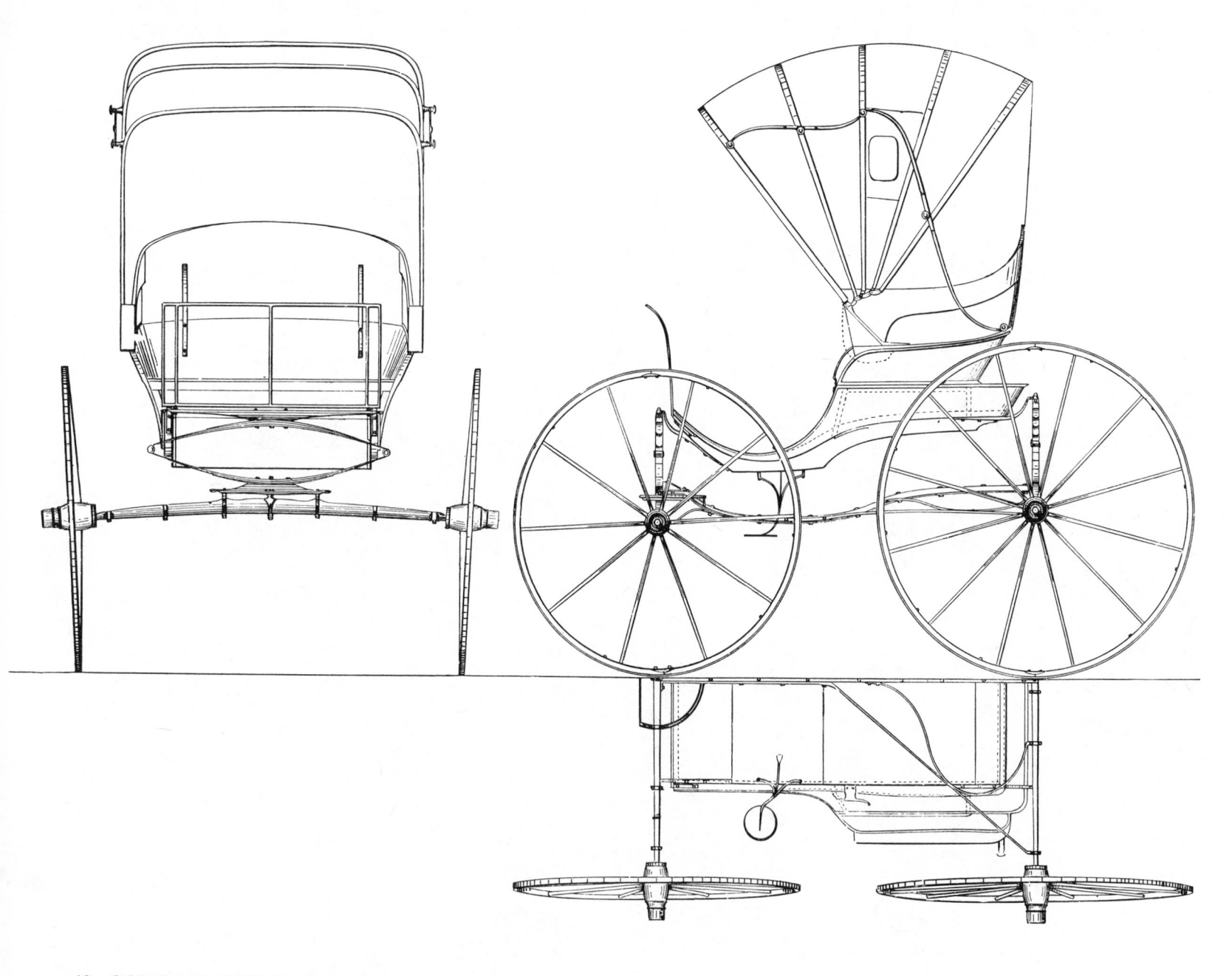

46. GODDARD BUGGY. A popular vehicle developed about the mid-1840s by the prominent Boston carriage builder, Thomas Goddard, it is almost phaeton-like in design. Black body and carriage. Carriage striped with three fine lines of cream white. Drab, blue, green, or maroon cloth trimmings, according to preference. Wheels 42″ and 46″. *The Hub,* vol. 22, Oct. 1880, p. 306.

47. STANHOPE BUGGY. This buggy borrowed its name and design from the earlier stanhope gig. A Studebaker quality vehicle, it had a genuine leather top with side curtains (not shown), and cost $295. Black body. Carriage either carmine striped black, or dark green striped red. Cloth, leather, or whipcord trimmings as preferred. Wheels 42″ and 46″. Catalog of the Studebaker Bros. Mfg. Co., South Bend, Ind. Dec. 1903.

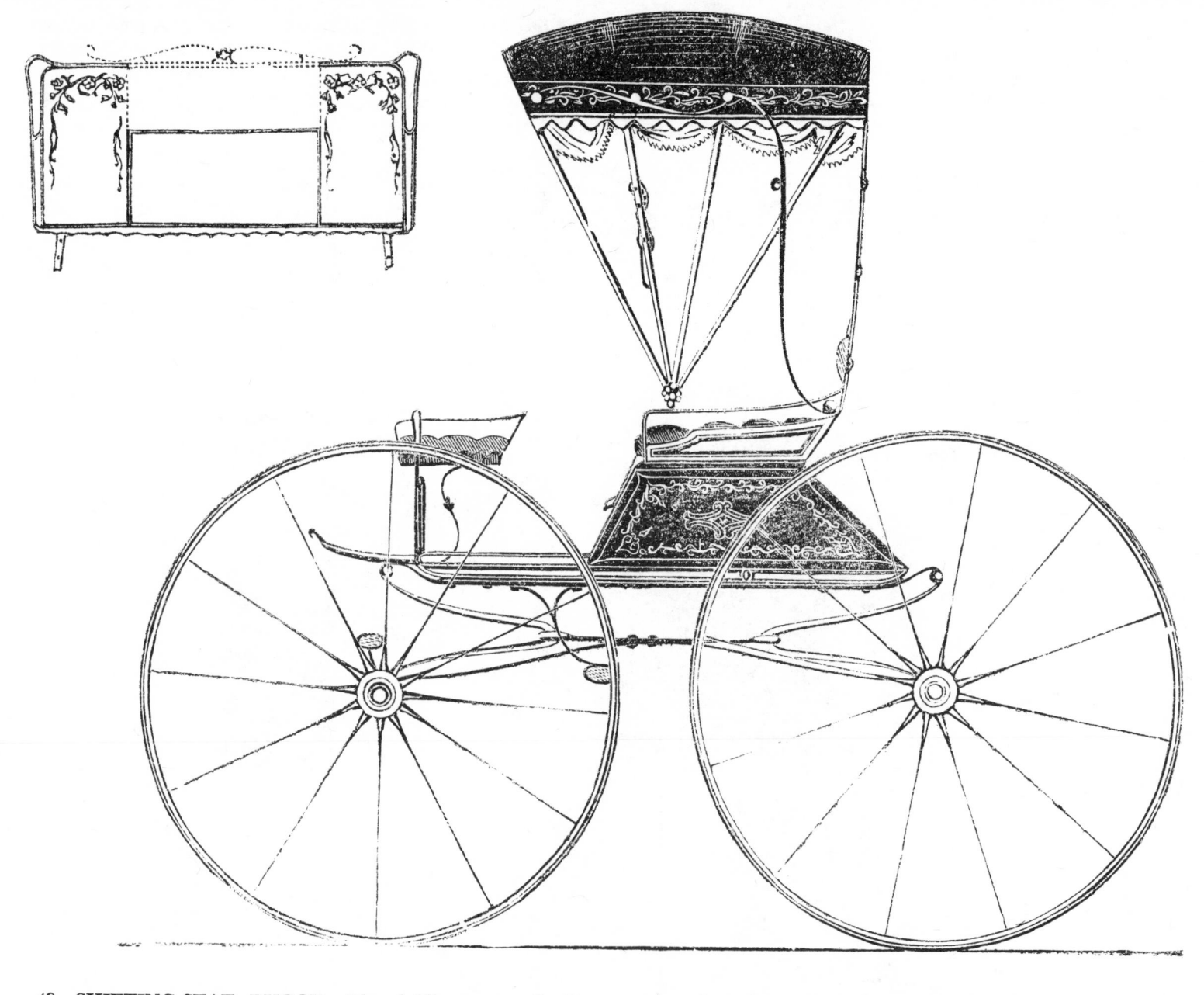

48. SHIFTING-SEAT BUGGY. The folding seat of this buggy converted it into a 3-passenger vehicle, since the shifting seat was only wide enough for one passenger. The footboard folded out of the way with the front seat, and the opening in the ornately stitched dash could then be closed with a leather-covered frame. Deep purple trimmings, with seat fall and cushion front of black patent leather. Light purple head lining and festoon curtains. Purple bodies on black carriages with gold and purple striping were sometimes seen at this time. *The Coach-maker's Magazine*, vol. 2, July 1856, pl. 18 (fig. 39).

49. CONCORD WAGON. A buggy invented in Concord, N.H. in about 1813 by Lewis Downing (builder of the Concord coach), its later versions were characterized by the three-perch carriage with side springs. (Perches are the longitudinal members of the running gear running from the rear axle to the head block.) Though a New England type, it was used throughout the country, particularly in the South. Black body, seat and moldings. Red seat moldings and imitation blinds. Red carriage with irons in black, but no striping. Gray whip-cord trimmings. Wheels 41″ and 46″. Track 56″. Body 45″ wide. *The Hub*, vol. 40, Mar. 1899, pl. 403.

50. DEARBORN WAGON. The original form of this wagon developed early in the 19th century, and was supposedly named because General Henry Dearborn used one in the field. The rear portion of the one shown here is enclosed by a curtain, like those in a rolled-up position on the front and middle sections. During the last quarter of the century this vehicle was also called a depot wagon. Black body. Olive green carriage striped black. Blue cloth trimming. Wheels 43″ and 48″. *The Carriage Monthly*, vol. 14, Feb. 1878, pl. 89.

51. DRIVING WAGON. Driving wagons were merely various types of buggies without tops and often with stick or spindle seats to create a lighter appearance. Black body. Carmine carriage striped black. Trimming of blue cloth, leather or whipcord. Wheels 42″ and 46″. Track 56″. Body 23″ by 56″ on bottom. Catalog of Studebaker Bros. Mfg. Co., South Bend, Ind., Dec. 1903.

52. DRIVING WAGON. This attractively styled model was popular with the ladies because of the cut-down front, which afforded easier access, and the rubber tires, which offered quieter and easier riding. Black body striped carmine. Carmine carriage striped black. *The Hub*, vol. 49, July 1907, pl. 812.

53. RUNABOUT. Essentially a buggy without a top, this vehicle was commonly known as a runabout, though the term "driving wagon", was often applied. Black body. Primrose-yellow carriage striped black. Green cloth trimming. Wheels 44″ and 49″. Track 56″. Body 37″ wide at the top of the seat. *The Hub*, vol. 34, Dec. 1892, pl. 49.

54. RUNABOUT. Just for variety, the Michigan Buggy Company called this cut-under runabout a "goabout." The cut-under feature permitted sharper turning in congested areas. Black body with green seat panels. Brewster green carriage with two 1/16″ stripes of carmine or yellow. Green cloth trimming. Wheels 38″ and 44″. Catalog of the Michigan Buggy Company, Kalamazoo, Mich., 1905.

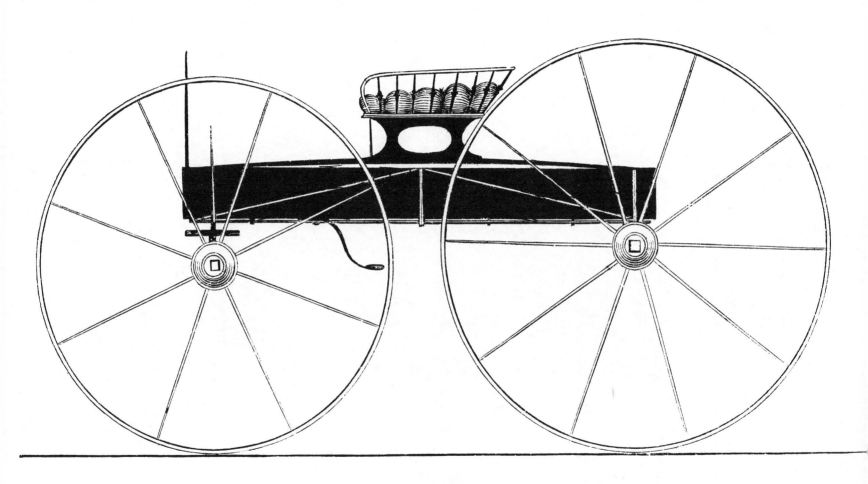

55. JAGGER WAGON. This popular wagon originated in the New York area. It featured an unsprung, square-box body set on bolsters, with a seat set on two wooden springs inside the body. It was a reasonably comfortable and economical vehicle. Wheels 46″ and 50″. *The New York Coach-maker's Magazine,* vol. 1, July 1858, pl. 5.

56. JAGGER WAGON. Later models featured improved suspension and canopy tops. By 1900 the name had become almost synonomous with "spring wagon" in some areas. Useful as family carriages, they were also extensively used as light business wagons. Black body. Black carriage with a medium stripe of green. Brown cloth trimming. Wheels 46½″ and 49″. Body 39″ wide at the top. *The Carriage Monthly*, vol. 18, April 1882, pl. 7.

57. JENNY LIND. In the mid-19th century a number of objects were named after the popular Swedish soprano, Jenny Lind. The carriage of that name was a variety of standing-top buggy. Wheels 47″ and 50″. *The New York Coach-maker's Magazine*, vol. 8, Aug. 1866, pl. 11.

58. JENNY LIND. Even after 1900 the Jenny Lind was still popular, particularly in smaller Pennsylvania towns. This one was built by S. E. Grosh & Co., of Lititz, Penna. Black body. Carmine carriage striped black. Dark green cloth trimming. Wheels 41″ and 44″. *The Carriage Monthly*, vol. 37, Mar. 1902, pl. 562.

59. ROAD WAGON. The name was often synonomous with "buggy." Most builders and dealers were likely to apply it to a buggy without a top, such as the popular stick-seat variety shown here. Black body. Carmine seat risers and pillars. Car-mine carriage striped with two lines of black. Light whipcord trimming. Wheels 40″ and 45″. Track 54″. Body 37″ wide across seat. *The Hub*, vol. 39, Feb. 1898, pl. 346.

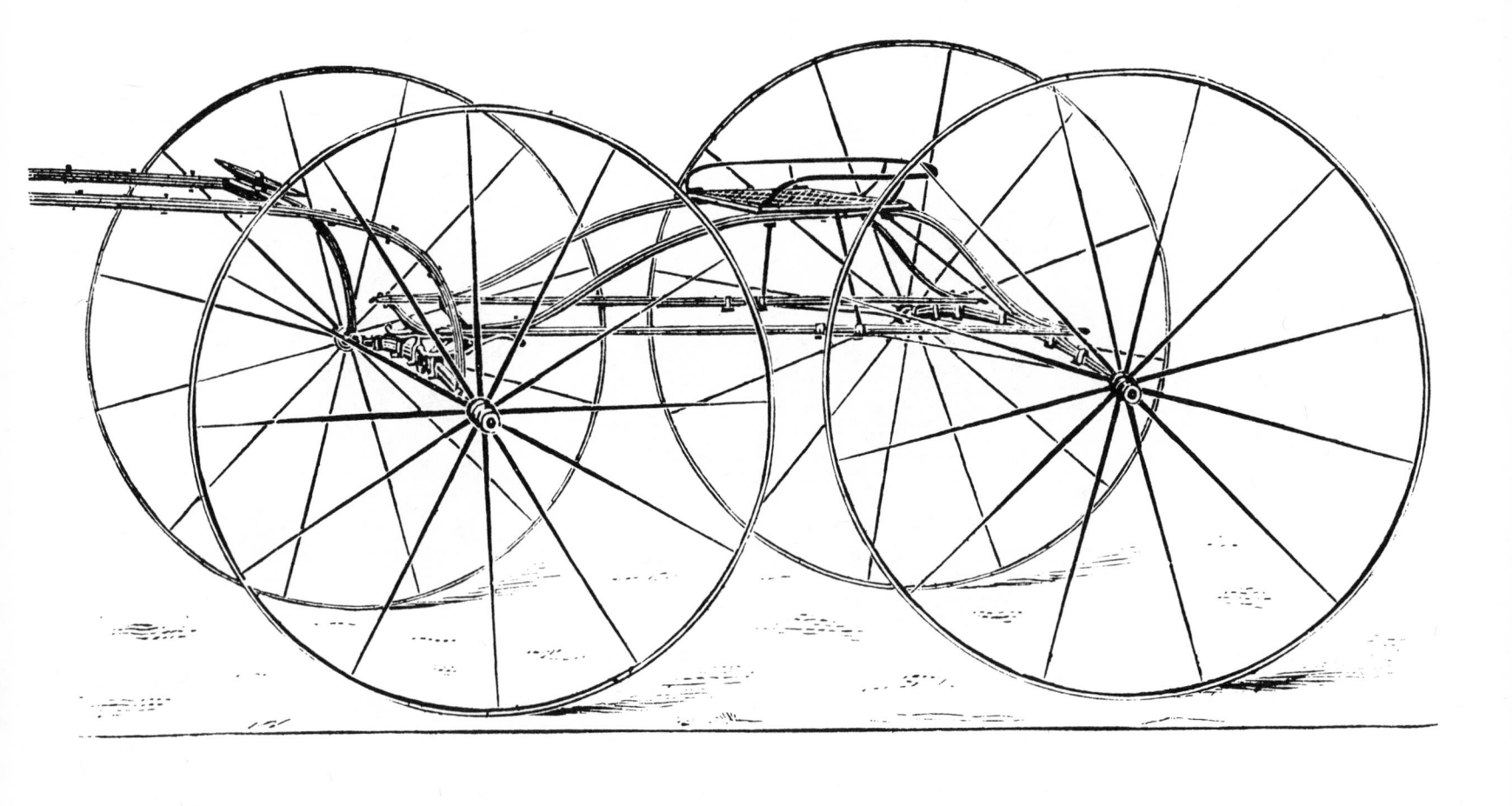

60. SKELETON WAGON. A trotting wagon intended for track use, this 59-pound vehicle pared down weight by using the hickory side bars for reaches. It was finished with a single coat of varnish. *The Hub*, vol. 18, July 1876, pl. 40.

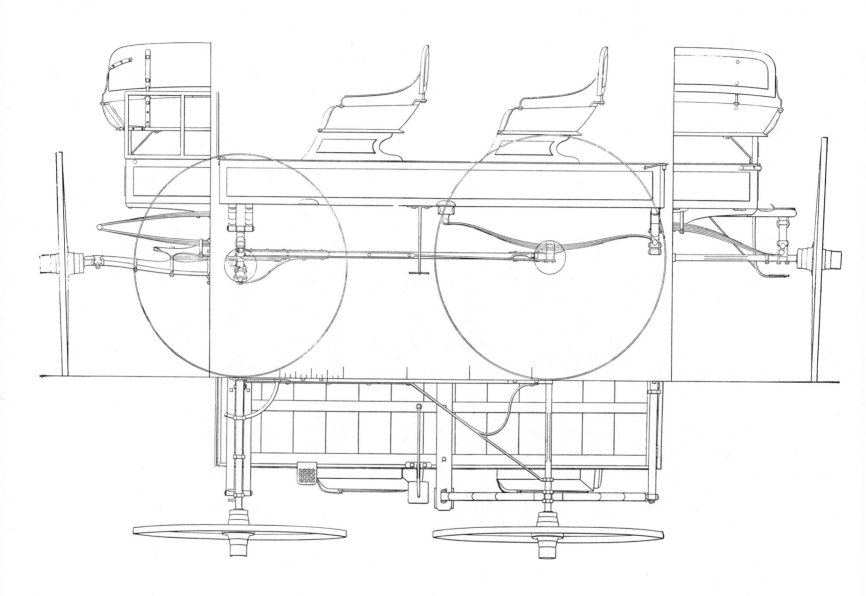

61. SPRING WAGON. An important vehicle in the late horse-drawn era was the spring wagon. Built with two to four removable seats, its practicality made it popular both in rural areas and in cities and towns where, with a single seat, it served as a business wagon. This model was known as a half-platform spring wagon because it used a perch and platform springs in the rear only. Black body with raised panels of deep green. Deep green carriage. Body and carriage striped carmine. Leather trimmings. *The Hub,* vol. 38, Sept. 1896, p. **392.**

62. SPRING WAGON. Manufactured by the Gate City Carriage Co., of Winona, Minn., this model was mounted on three elliptics and had no platform springs. Black body striped red. Deep vermilion carriage striped black. Green cloth trimming. Wheels 39″ and 44″. *The Carriage Monthly*, vol. 34, March 1899, pl. 83.

63. SPRING WAGON. Many spring wagons such as this one on duplex springs, had canopy tops. Equipped with optional pole or shafts for use with one or two horses, it cost $54.50 in 1907. Black body with deep green seat risers. Dark Brewster green carriage. Body and carriage striped red. Black leather or imitation leather trimming, the genuine leather costing $4 more. Catalog of the Elkhart Carriage and Harness Mfg. Co., Elkhart, Ind., 1907.

64. DEMOCRAT WAGON. This was nothing but a spring wagon under another popular name which suggested the vehicle's modest and democratic character. It has been slightly refined in this model by rounded corners and a cut-down front which affords easier access. Wheels 42″ and 50″. Body 39″ wide. *The Hub,* vol. 17, Jan. 1876, p. 334.

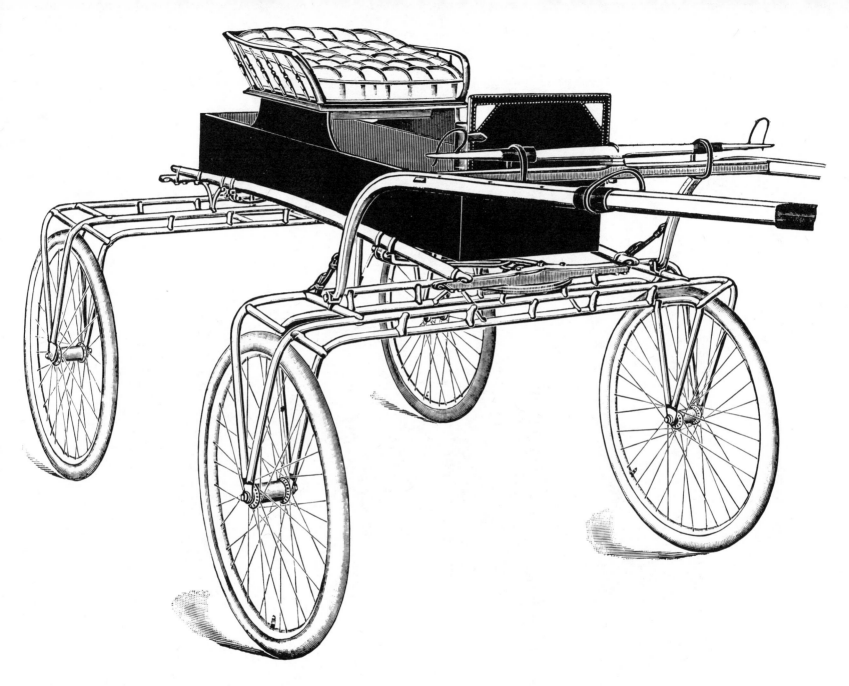

65. SPEEDING WAGON. Light and fast, the speeding wagon was a type of driving wagon usually built for a single passenger. It was sometimes used at horse shows. This one, by the George Werner firm, of Buffalo, N.Y., was mounted on springs. It weighed 94 pounds with springs; 75 pounds without. Pneumatic tires were mounted on wire wheels. Black body on a carmine carriage, striped black. Whipcord trimming. *The Carriage Monthly,* vol. 37, Dec. 1901, pl. 526.

66. WHITECHAPEL WAGON. In 1872 James Brewster & Co., of New York City, placed the body of the English Whitechapel cart on the carriage of a road wagon, resulting in what might be called a Whitechapel buggy. Dark green body panels. Chamfers of ribs striped black. Face of ribs striped orange. Black carriage with three fine orange stripes. Dark green cloth trimming. Wheels 44″ and 47″. Seat frame 31″ wide. *The Hub,* vol. 22, June 1880, pl. 30.

67. SURREY. Soon the Whitechapel wagon came to be known as a surrey wagon, or surrey. During the earlier part of the vehicle's history it was built for two or four passengers. This one, built by Pease, Perrine & Co., of Fremont, Ohio, features a lowered suspension by means of a drop-perch. Black body and carriage. Carriage striped red. Green cloth trimming. Wheels 44″ and 48″. *The Carriage Monthly*, vol. 16, Oct. 1880, pl. 53.

68. SURREY. Still showing the distinct lines of a White-chapel, this surrey carried four passengers, a factor that soon made it one of the most popular low-price family carriages. The front seat was divided in the center to allow one half to turn over, for access to the rear. Surries might have standing tops, falling tops, umbrella tops, or no top at all. Dark green body, with black moldings. Carriage, a lighter shade of green with two fine stripes of black. Green cloth trimming. Wheels 44″ and 47″. *The Hub*, vol. 24, April 1882, pl. 7.

69. SURREY. Here, with sides cut down for easier access, is the typical, fully developed surrey with its fringed canopy top. In the early 1900s such vehicles could be purchased for $50 to $100. Deep blue body. Light blue dusters, moldings and small upper seat panels. Molding with a single stripe of cream. Deep blue carriage striped cream. Dark blue cloth trimming. Wheels 38″ and 44″. *The Hub*, vol. 36, April 1894, pl. 73.

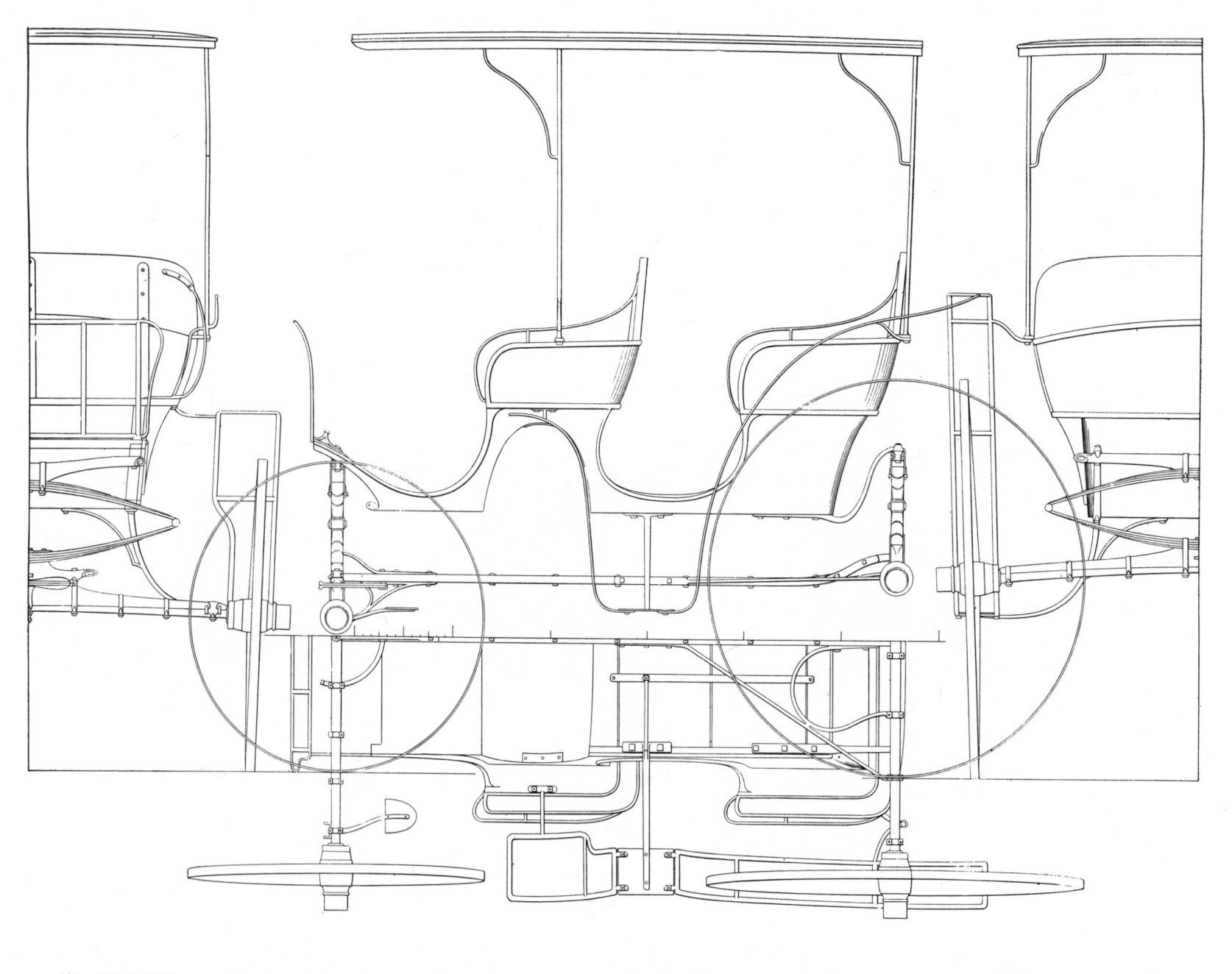

70. SURREY. Another variety of surrey features the cut-under body, allowing the front wheels to be turned sharply under the body. Most canopy tops could be removed if desired. Some surries had fenders of patent leather on iron frames, made in the same manner as the dash. *The Hub*, vol. 36, Jan. 1895, p. 730.

71. BREAK. A sporting vehicle that was used for hunting parties and picnics, this variety of break incorporated some of the features of a dog cart. This model, the height of its sides relieved by canework, could carry eight passengers, dogs under the rear seats and food and ammunition under the front seat. Wheels 38″ and 47″. *The New York Coach-maker's Magazine,* vol. 5, Mar. 1864, pl. 36.

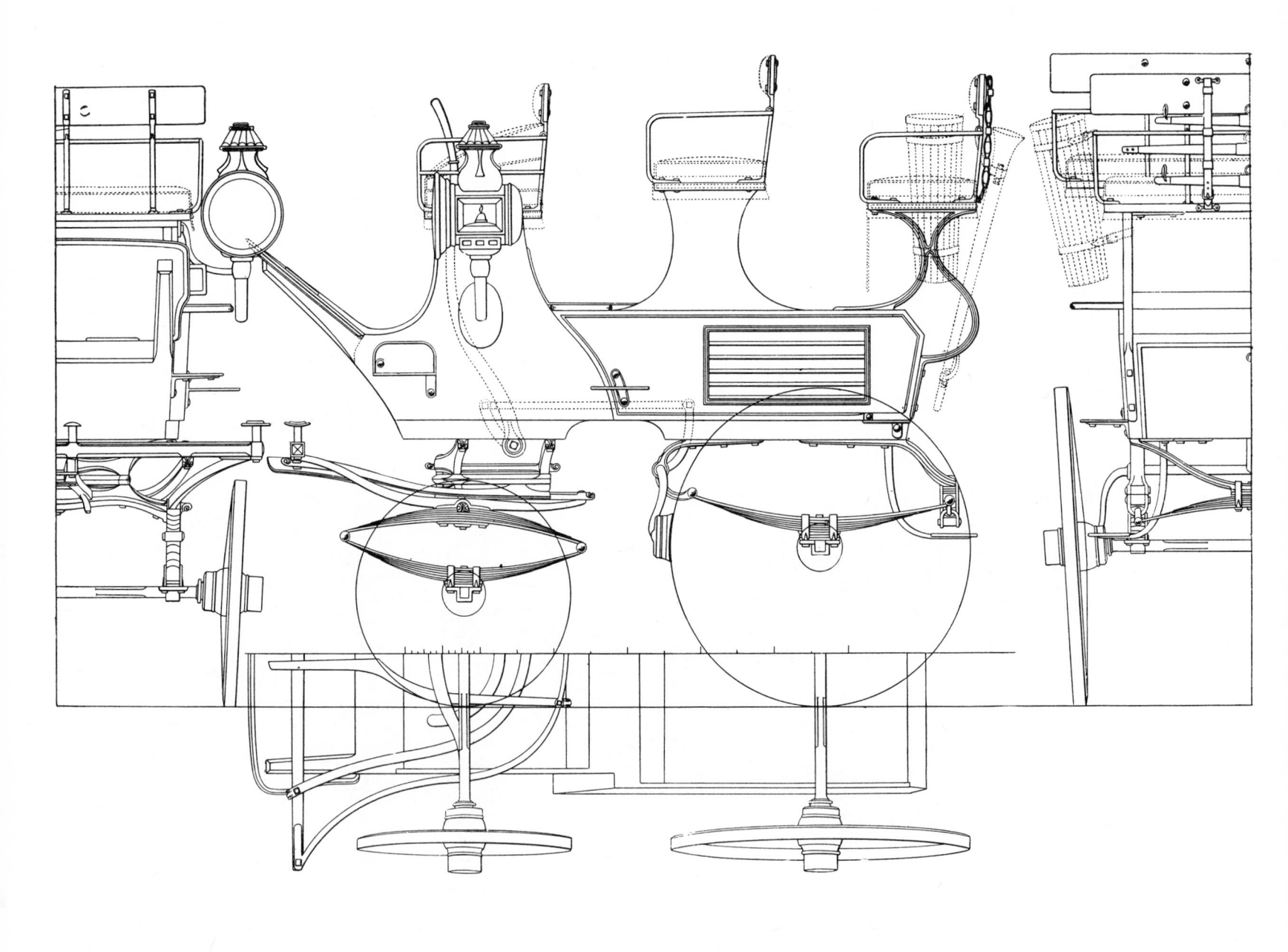

72. BREAK. A heavier model, carrying nine passengers (two in front, four in center and three in the rear) was also equipped for under-seat stowage and, in this instance, louvered ventilation for the dogs. Black body with red louvers and rockers. Red carriage with a broad black stripe. Drab corduroy trimming. Horn-case and umbrella-basket of wickerwork. *The Hub*, vol. 36, April 1894, p. 28.

73. PHAETON. A phaeton equipped with a standing top could be comfortably enclosed in inclement weather by rolling down the curtains. A charcoal-burning foot warmer might add its warmth to the passengers' comfort. (Photo from Smithsonian Institution.)

74. DROP-FRONT PHAETON. The lowered floor of this phaeton, giving the vehicle its name, helps to create a low-hung carriage which affords easy access. This one, in the collection of the Smithsonian Institution, was built about 1860. Carriages of this type were popular among doctors, who frequently had the sides of the falling top enclosed for privacy and added protection against inclement weather. Black body and carriage. Carriage with fine stripes of yellow and green. Wheels 42″ and 48″. (Photo from Smithsonian Institution.)

Center Line.

1 INCH SCALE.   0   1   2   3   4   5   6   7

75. DROP-FRONT PHAETON. Unlike the Smithsonian's model, mounted on two elliptic springs, this one, by D. M. Lane's Sons of Philadelphia, is suspended on scroll-end platform springs that complement the scroll-end body loops. Deep green body and carriage. Body with one yellow stripe; carriage with two. Dark green cloth trimming. Wheels 38″ and 48″. *The Carriage Monthly,* vol. 30, Sept. 1894, p. 171.

76. EXTENSION-TOP PHAETON. This was a popular, practical, and moderately economical family carriage. Seen here is the "gypsy top," so-called because of the pattern of the triangular side quarters. Many had open sides, rather than the low doors of this example. Wheels 40″ and 48″. *The Coachmakers' Magazine*, vol. 2, Aug. 1856, pl. 19, fig. 42.

77. EXTENSION-TOP PHAETON. This attractive model is mounted on platform springs in the rear and on an elliptic spring in front. Iron-frame, leather-covered fenders help to protect the carriage and occupants from mud. In lowering the top, it was first necessary to insert the pivots of the front set of top bows into the eyes on the forward bow of the rear set.

The ornamented straps hanging down next to the rear light held the curtain when it was rolled up. Dark green seat panels. Black moldings striped light green. Black rockers, Green carriage with two stripes of lighter green and one of carmine. Light-colored whipcord trimming. Wheels 34″ and 46″. Body 44″ wide. *The Hub*, vol. 40, Aug. 1898, pl. 379.

78. BASKET PHAETON. Originating in England, the basket phaeton became popular in America for park and beach use. A wood and iron framework was completed with willow bas- ketwork. This model has a rumble for a servant. Wheels 30″ and 36″. *The New York Coach-maker's Magazine*, vol. 6, Sept. 1864, pl. 14.

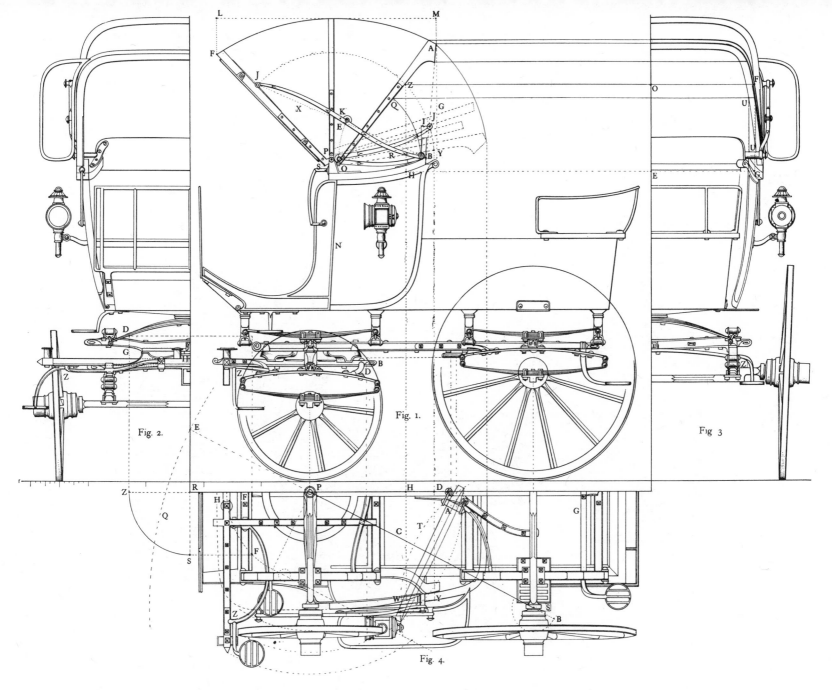

79. MAIL PHAETON. In about 1830 English carriage-builders applied the suspension of the mail coach to a new style of sporting phaeton. The use of the mail spring gave rise to the term "mail phaeton." It was used not only as a sporting vehicle, but also as a gentleman's driving carriage, and sometimes as a traveling carriage. The rear seat was intended for servants. *The Hub*, vol. 45, Dec. 1903, p. 332.

80. STANHOPE PHAETON. A lighter version of the mail phaeton, the vehicle took its name from the curved-panel front seat with a stanhope pillar (the outline of the front seat, down to the floor). The lighter build often allowed the use of elliptic springs. This one was equipped for pair-horse draught, but some were used with a single horse. Black body. Dark green seat panels. Black moldings with a fine stripe of light green. Dark green carriage with a heavy stripe and two medium stripes of black. Trimming of green morocco for backs and cushions, and of green cloth for other parts. Wheels 34″ and 45″. Front seat 45″ wide. Track 54″. *The Hub*, vol. 27, Dec. 1885, pl. 70.

81. QUEEN'S-BODY PHAETON. All ladies' phaetons were light and low, but this variety was further characterized by a curving bottom line. Cobalt blue body and carriage. Black moldings and arm rail. Carriage with two fine stripes of chrome yellow. Blue cloth trimming. Gold mountings. Wheels 37″ and 46″. Track 54″. Body 40″ wide. *The Hub*, vol. 17, Sept. 1875, p. 184.

82. SPIDER PHAETON. An American innovation of about 1861, the spider phaeton (essentially a Tilbury body on four wheels) reached its greatest popularity during the last decade of the century. It was a gentleman's carriage, with a skeleton rumble for a groom. It was also an effective vehicle for horse-show work. Black panels. Blue moldings and stanhope pillar, with a fine stripe of canary yellow. Black carriage with a broad stripe of light blue distanced with two fine stripes of canary yellow. Blue cloth trimming. Wheels 35″ and 41″. Track 52″. Body 44″ wide. *The Hub,* vol. 29, April 1887, pl. 3.

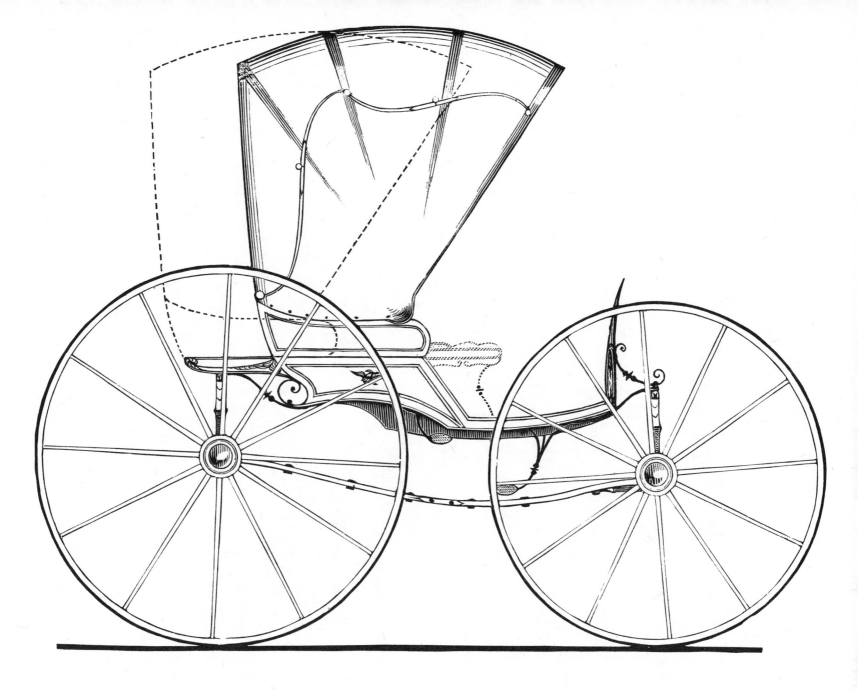

83. SLIDING-SEAT PHAETON. A popular feature at mid-century was the sliding seat, allowing a buggy of phaeton to accommodate either two or four passengers. This attractive phaeton was convertible in the manner shown by the dotted lines. The main seat slid back onto the pump handles and the upholstered seat-fall turned up to become an extra seat supported by pivoted iron legs. Wheels 44″ and 48″. *The Coach-makers' Magazine*, vol. 3, June 1857, pl. 21.

84. GEORGE IV PHAETON. The fashionable George IV phaeton was a highly popular carriage for ladies' driving, for its design was well adapted to show off the ladies' costume. The splinter-bar in front, supporting two sets of roller-bolts (the posts in front, to which the traces are attached), indicates that it was intended for pair-horse driving. From *Driving for Pleasure*, by Francis T. Underhill. D. Appleton & Co., N.Y., 1896, plate LXVI.

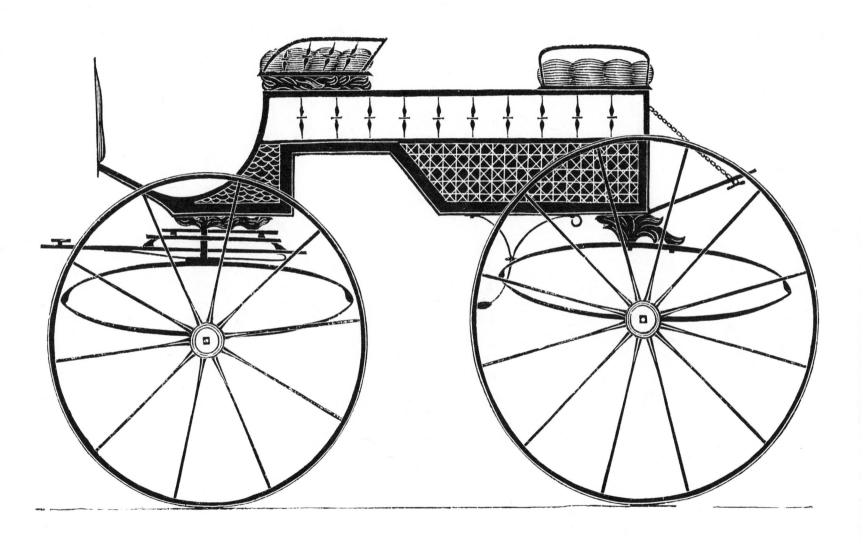

85. DOG-CART PHAETON. Though often called a dog cart, the application of the term "cart" to a four-wheel vehicle is incorrect; "dog-cart phaeton" is a more proper usage. Here the dog cart has been lengthened and a cut-under has been provided to allow the wheels to turn sharply. The front cane-work is imitation; that on the rear is real. Dark blue body. Cream-color carriage. Wheels 43″ and 47″. *The New York Coach-maker's Magazine*, vol. 3, July 1860, pl. 6.

86. DOG-CART PHAETON. Suggestive of the trap of a later era, the vehicle had a rear seat that folded out of sight. All passengers faced forward in this carriage. Wheels 44″ and 48″.

Catalog of Lawrence, Bradley and Pardee, New Haven, Conn. 1862.

87. TRAP. A carriage similar to this was in use in America by the mid-19th century, but was known by such names as "dog-cart phaeton" and "sliding-seat wagon." About 1892 the term "trap," previously used in a somewhat loose manner, began to be applied. Studebaker called this one a hunting trap. Catalog of the Studebaker Bros. Mfg. Co., South Bend, Ind., 1893.

88. TRAP. Although traps varied considerably in construction, most shared the feature of having one or more movable seats, so that the vehicle could be converted from two- to four-passenger capacity. Sometimes a rear seat could be made to face either forward or backward. In this model the rear seat was designed so it could be folded entirely into the body, giving the carriage a light, sporty look. White imitation cane-work. Vermilion side medallion, seat, back panel and toeboard bottom. Black molding. Vermilion carriage striped black. Light Bedford cord trimming. Wheels 44″ and 47″. Track 54″. Seat width 36″. *The Hub,* vol. 38, June 1896, pl. 234.

89. TRAP. A rather common style had a divided front seat built so that one side could be turned outward for access to the rear seat. Body black, except for the narrow carmine panel. Body striped gold. Carmine carriage striped gold. Leather trimming. Wheels 40″ and 44″. Track 56″. Seat 36½″ wide at the top. *The Hub*, vol. 38, Mar. 1897, pl. 284.

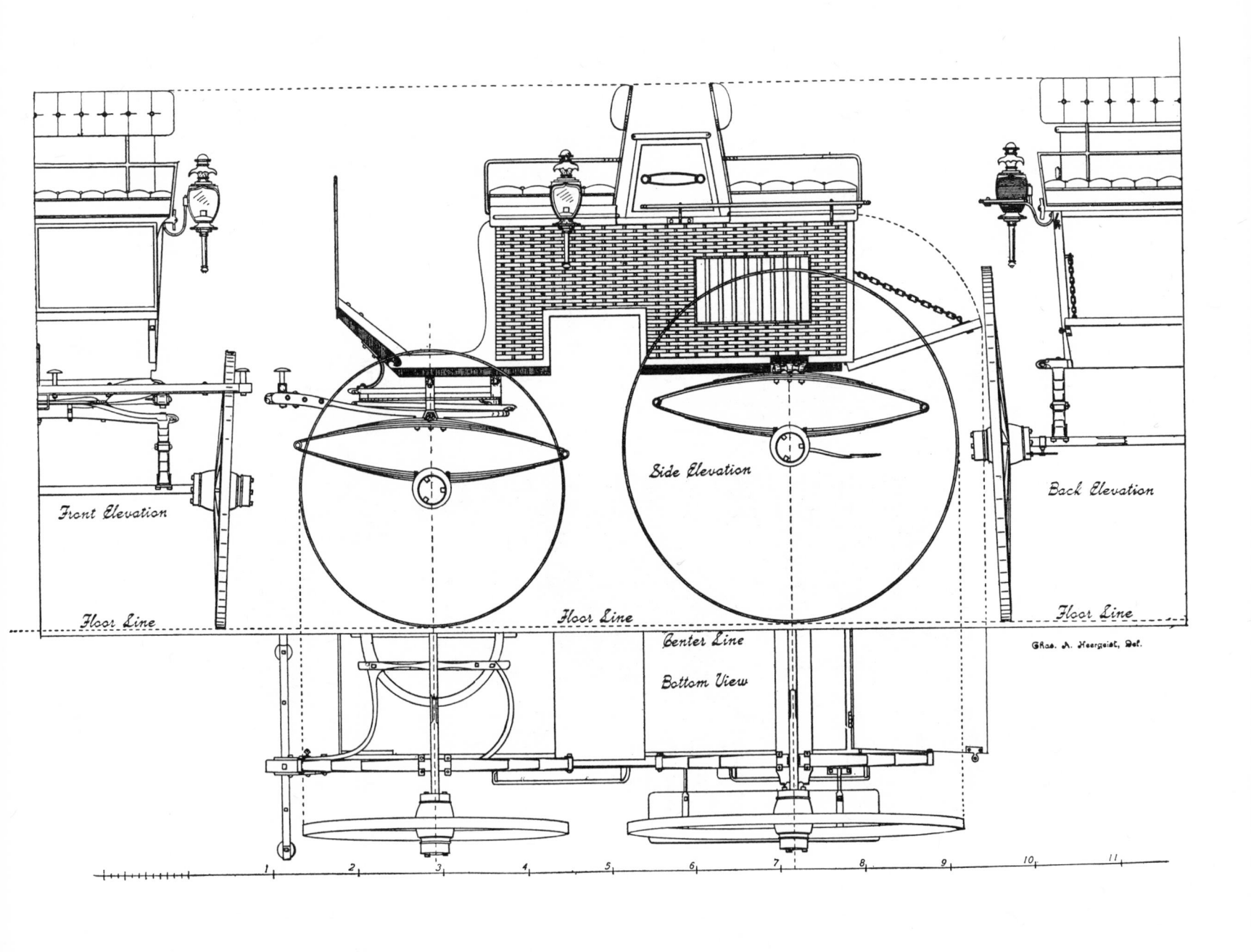

Front Elevation

Side Elevation

Back Elevation

Floor Line

Floor Line

Floor Line

Center Line

Bottom View

Chas. A. Heergeist, Del.

1 2 3 4 5 6 7 8 9 10 11

90. TRAP. Another fairly common style had a back seat facing the rear and an endgate that was let down to serve as a toeboard when the rear seat was in use. The picnic locker indicates the intended use of this model. *The Carriage Monthly*, vol. 35, June 1899, p. 72.

91. GERMANTOWN. Known variously as a Germantown, a Germantown wagon, or a Germantown rockaway, this popular family carriage borrowed features from the earlier coaches, and, in later years, often borrowed the name of the rockaway, even though it predated that carriage. The Germantown originated in about 1816 in Germantown, Pa., and continued to be built until the 1880s. Wheels 44″ and 50″. *The Coachmakers' Magazine*, vol. 3, Oct. 1857, pl. 33.

THE HUB N.Y.

92. CURTAIN ROCKAWAY. The rockaway was a convenient and practical family carriage. Because of the cover provided for the driver, it is said to have been representative of a democratic society. It seems more likely that the concern for the driver's comfort might be attributed to the fact that he was often the head of the household, though the rockaway was also frequently servant-driven. The curtain rockaway was a common type, having movable glasses in the front and in the doors while the rear quarters and back were closed by the curtains that can be seen rolled at the top. Body and carriage with a natural wood finish. Drab corduroy trimmings. Wheel 37″ and 47″. Track 56″. Body 50″ wide on top. *The Hub*, vol. 33, July 1891, pl. 24.

93. COUPE ROCKAWAY. Of American origin, the rockaway was a popular carriage. Its ancestral form was built in about 1830 at Jamaica, Long Island. Several features embodied in its design were evidently borrowed from the earlier coachee and the Germantown. This coupé rockaway combines the features of the coupé with the covered driver's seat of the rockaway. Glasses in the doors and front were made to drop.

Purple body panels. Belt and other parts, black. Belt moldings (those at about seat level, forming the "belt" around the carriage) with fine gold stripe. Black carriage with ⅜″ purple stripe edged with gold or canary yellow. Brown cloth trimming. Wheels 40″ and 48″. Track 60″. Body 44″ wide. *Coachmaker's International Journal*, vol. 4, Jan. 1869, pl. 14.

94. LIGHT ROCKAWAY. The vehicle had no glasses, but was entirely enclosed by curtains. It could be drawn by one or two horses. Lower part of the body and front seat panels, deep green. Black moldings. Deep green carriage with fine stripes of pale green. Green cloth trimming. Wheels 36″ and 46″. Body 43″ wide at back of door. *The Carriage Monthly,* vol. 30, May 1894, pl. 14.

95. EXTENSION-FRONT ROCKAWAY. The largest of the rockaways was the extension-front, or six-passenger rockaway. This one is entirely enclosed by glass, but others were partly or entirely enclosed by curtains. Deep green doors, rear quarter panels and S-pillars. Balance black. Moldings striped with olive green. Deep green carriage striped with olive green. Goatskin trimmings. Green satin curtains. Wheels 36″ and 52″. Track 56″. *The Hub,* vol. 36, Feb. 1895, pl. 136.

96. ROCKALET. A less common carriage than the rockaway was the rockalet. It combined the body of a rockaway with a folding rear portion of the top similar to a landaulet. The carriage could not be converted while on the road; when the rear part was folded down, the front portion had to be lifted off and left at home. Black body with dark green panels. Dark green carriage with two 3/16″ white stripes. Green cloth and morocco trimmings. Wheels 36″ and 48″. Body 47″ wide at back of door. *The Carriage Monthly*, vol. 23, May 1887, pl. 10.

97. DEPOT WAGON. The depot wagon appears to have developed from the Dearborn wagon around the mid-19th century. As its name suggests, it was a practical vehicle for carrying travelers and their luggage from train depots. The seats of this one were made to slide on rails to accommodate luggage more readily. It was also a comfortable and versatile vehicle for family use. Wheels 47″ and 50″. Body 49″ wide. *The New York Coach-maker's Magazine*, vol. 5, May 1864, pl. 44.

98. DEPOT WAGON. The vehicle eventually acquired some of the characteristics of the rockaway, which, like the Dearborn, had a standing top that also covered the driver's seat. Black body. Lake carriage with two stripes of carmine. Brown cloth trimming. Wheels 39″ and 48″. Track 56″. Body 36″ wide on top. Seats 41½″ on top. *The Hub,* vol. 27, Sept. 1885, pl. 45.

99. DEPOT WAGON. In its final development, the depot wagon was essentially a modified rockaway, this one resembling a curtain rockaway. Only the squared rear quarters distinguish it from the rockaway, thus preserving the "wagon" features. Deep green body. Front seat panel and imitation blinds a lighter green. Black moldings striped with carmine. Carmine carriage with two black stripes. Blue cloth trimming. Wheels 36″ and 46″. Track 56″. Body 45″ wide at hinge pillars (the pillars to which the hinges are attached). *The Hub,* vol. 38, July 1896, pl. 239.

100. DEPOT WAGON. A light depot wagon, or station wagon, served the needs of a small hotel by meeting guests at the rail repot, whereas a larger hotel might have used a wagonette or an omnibus. (Photo from Smithsonian Institution.)

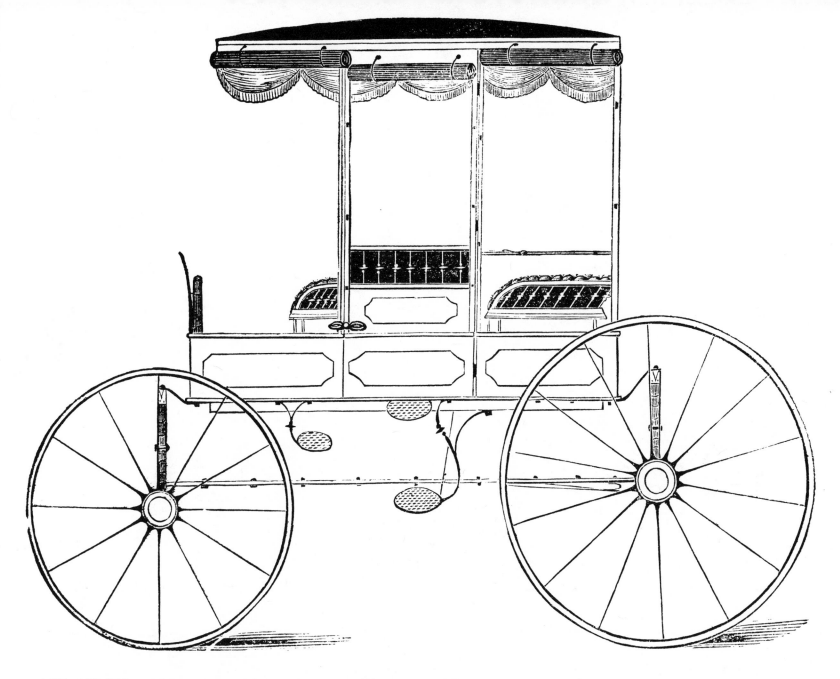

101. JERSEY WAGON. Commonly employed as a family carriage and as a traveling wagon, the Jersey wagon was used from the late 18th century until almost the end of the horse-drawn era. This one bears some resemblance to a rockaway or a depot wagon. Its seats could be moved about or removed entirely. This wagon was most frequently seen in New Jersey and eastern Pennsylvania. Main panels umber. Smaller center panels light lake. Black moldings. Wheels 42″ and 49″. *The Coach-makers' Magazine*, vol. 1, May 1885, pl. 9.

102. JAUNTING WAGON. This is an Americanized version, on four wheels, of the Irish jaunting car. Built by the Parsons Vehicle Co. of Columbus, Ohio, it carried two persons on each side seat and two on the front. It was intended for use in summer resort areas, and for small outing parties. There is no evidence that it ever gained much acceptance. Black body. Carmine toeboards striped black. Carmine carriage with no striping. Bedford cord trimming. Wheels 36″ and 44″. Front seat 36″ wide. *The Hub*, vol. 43, Nov. 1901, pl. 531.

103. BERLIN COACH. Although strictly speaking the term "Berlin" refers to a 17th-century running gear or undercarriage, it was occasionally applied, inappropriately, to 19th-century coaches. Here it was used at the whim of the builder because the upper rear quarters were fitted with glasses instead of panels. Lower panels of body, deep green. Upper part of body and boot, black. Carriage deep green with three ¼" lemon yellow stripes. Green morocco and cloth trimming. Wheels 38" and 46". *The Carriage Monthly*, vol. 23, Jan. 1888, pl. 83.

104. BRETT. James Goold & Co., of Albany, New York, originators of the famed Albany cutter, built this carriage. The back of the front passenger seat was hinged to fold down, forming a cover to the seat. Dark green body with black moldings. Black carriage striped with red. Green cloth trimming. Wheels 39″ and 48″. *The New York Coach-maker's Magazine,* vol. 1, Jan. 1859, pl. 28.

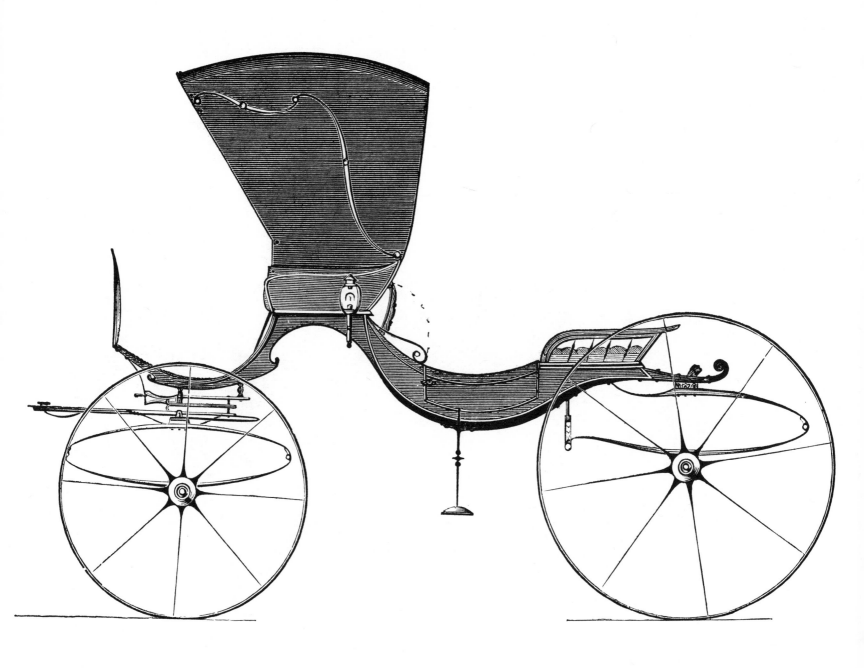

105. CONVERTIBLE BRETT. The front and rear seats could be switched, putting the calash top over the front seat, as shown here. Wheels 40″ and 48″. Catalog of Lawrence, Bradley and Pardee, New Haven, Connecticut, 1862, pl. 149.

106. EXTENSION-TOP BRETT. Later bretts had a forward passenger seat with a fixed back and an extension top that covered both passenger seats. Bottle-green body panels. Black moldings with a fine line of yellow on the edge. Bottle-green carriage with two yellow stripes. Green cloth trimming. Wheels 36″ and 46″. Body 46″ wide at top. *The Hub*, vol. 30, April 1888, pl. 3.

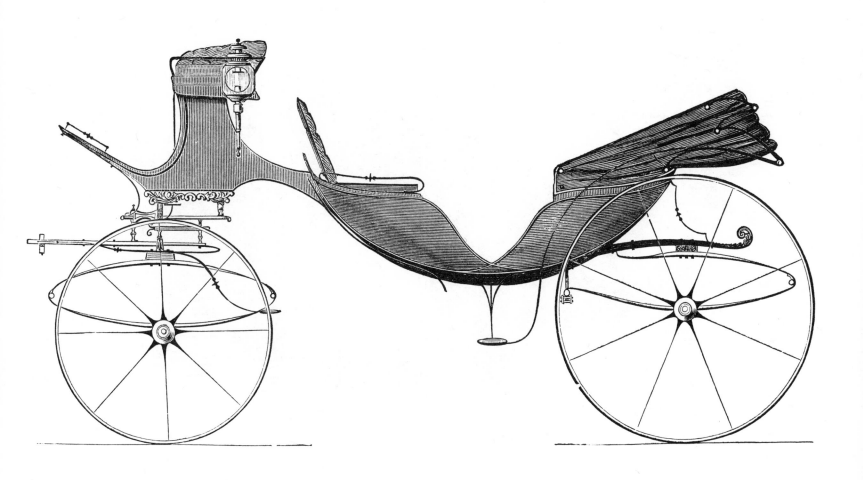

107. GLADSTONE. The Gladstone differed from the brett by having no half-doors. Wheels 40″ and 48″. Catalog of Lawrence, Bradley & Pardee, New Haven, Conn., 1862, Plate **139.**

108. COACH. The coach was a vehicle of the wealthy, costing from $1000 to $1300 during the mid-19th century. At the rear is the small page-board in the raised position. The tassel-ornamented footman-holders steadied the servant as he stood on the lowered page-board. Wheels 40″ and 48″. *The New York Coach-maker's Magazine,* vol. 3, Oct. 1860, pl. 16.

109. COACH. The coach was also made with glasses in the upper quarters for those who wished a better view of the passing scenery. Dark blue lower quarters, doors and back panels. Black moldings on upper quarters and back panels. Dark blue carriage with two narrow yellow stripes. Blue goatskin trimming for cushions and backs; blue satin for the other parts. Wheels 36″ and 45″. Body 53″ wide. *The Hub*, vol. 26, Dec. 1884, pl. 72.

110. FALLING-FRONT COACH. This coach, by Kean and Lines of New Haven, Conn., is really a half-landau because of the falling front. Black moldings, upper part of body and boot. Deep green lower panels. Moldings with a fine stripe of light green. Deep green carriage with three stripes of light green. Green morocco and cloth trimmings. Silver mountings. Wheels 38″ and 46″. *The Carriage Monthly*, vol. 23, Sept. 1887, pl. 49.

111. DRAWING-ROOM COACH. James Goold & Co., of Albany, N.Y., built this unusual coach. It could be made into an open vehicle with very little effort by sliding the quarter lights together with the standing pillars into the quarters, while the door lights could be dropped into the doors. Black body and carriage. Carriage striped tan, distanced with fine red stripes. Brown morocco trimmings. Roof and quarters trimmed with brown satin. Wheels 41″ and 49″. Body 51″ wide. *The Hub,* vol. 18, July 1876, p. 121.

112. CLARENCE. Although the clarence was very similar to a coach, in reality it was an extra large coupé, with a semi-circular front enclosed either by glass or a panel, and containing a full-framed seat facing the rear seat. Clarences were expensive, in the late 1860s they were likely to cost $1700 to $2000. Brown body and carriage. Carriage with three stripes of deep orange. Brown satin or Bismark-brown trimming. Wheels 43″ and 47″. Body 54″ wide. *The New York Coachmaker's Magazine,* vol. 11, June 1869, pl. 1.

113. CLARENCE. The other type of clarence had a paneled front instead of glass. Wheels 42″ and 46″. *The New York*   *Coach-maker's Magazine*, vol. 8, Sept. 1866, pl. 13.

114. LANDAU. The Landau originated in Germany during the first half of the 18th century. Actually a coach with a falling top, it was one of the last heavy carriages to pass from use, lasting until the advent of the automobile. This model is suspended on both elliptic and C-springs. Black body and carriage. Carriage with a ⅜″ stripe of blue with 2 narrow white stripes overlaid near the edges. Wheels 41″ and 49″. *The New York Coach-maker's Magazine*, vol. 11, Apr. 1870, pl. 41.

115. ENGLISH-QUARTER LANDAU. Heavy and complicated owing to the falling top, and consequently expensive, the landau was a carriage of the wealthy. This example, by the famed Brewster & Co., of Broome St., New York City, was characterized by the drop-center and angular lines. It was exhibited at the Centennial Exhibition in Philadelphia.

Lake panels. Black moldings and boot. Lake carriage with a broad black stripe and 2 fine stripes of New York red. Maroon morocco and cloth trimming. Driver's seat of maroon cloth welted with black leather. Wheels 36″ and 48″. *The Hub*, vol. 18, July 1876, pl. 46.

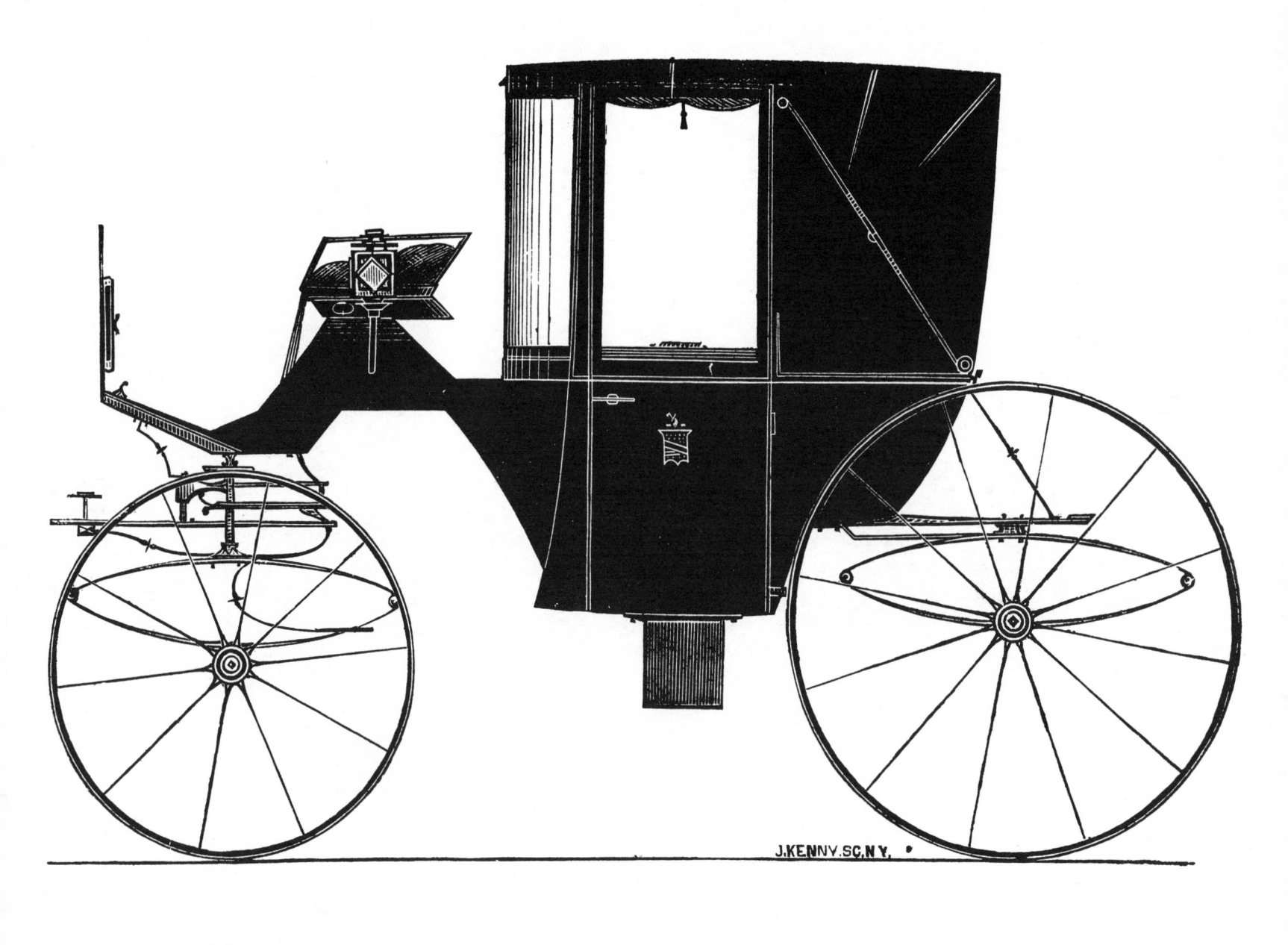

116. LANDAULETTE. The laudaulette was basically a chariot or coupé with a falling top. Like the landau, it was a luxury vehicle. Wheels 39″ and 48″. Body 48″ wide at the door. *The New York Coach-maker's Magazine*, vol. 12, Jan. 1871, pl. 29.

117. LANDAULETTE. Many models had round or octagon fronts, which made lowering the top a troublesome task, since the front had to be folded or dropped before the top was lowered. Chocolate brown body. Black boot, panels and moldings. Moldings edged with a fine stripe of deep orange. Chocolate brown carriage striped black, edged with a fine stripe of deep orange. Brown morocco and brown satin trimmings. Driver's cushion of brown cloth. Wheels 36″ and 45″. Body 50″ wide at the hinge pillars. *The Hub*, vol. 25, Feb. 1884, pl. 91.

118. BAROUCHE. This carriage was essentially a landau with half of a falling top and an unprotected front passenger seat. Some had extension-tops, others a hinged back to the front seat, making them indistinguishable from the brett. The sides above the quarters and doors of this example were carved in imitation of basketwork and were surrounded by silver moldings. Wheels 42″ and 48″. *The New York Coachmaker's Magazine*, vol. 2, July 1859, pl. 6.

119. BAROUCHE. In presenting this plate, *The Carriage Monthly* said that the vehicle was, by 1880 generally known as a phaeton (either half-top or extension-top) or brett, the term "barouche" having passed from use. Dark green body. Sage green carriage with two ¼″ stripes of malori green. Green cloth trimming. Wheels 35″ and 46″. Body 41″ wide. *The Carriage Monthly,* vol. 15, Jan. 1880, pl. 78.

120. BROUGHAM. This type of vehicle, which originated in London about 1839, was intended as a gentleman's carriage. It also became extremely popular as a public cab in both England and America. The angular lines, and door clos-ing to the bottom line, make this a Peters-type brougham, originated by Peters & Sons, of London. *The Hub*, vol. 32, Oct. 1890, pl. 52.

121. DORSAY or DOUBLE-SUSPENSION BROUGHAM.
Named after Count D'Orsay, the term was used for a coupé or brougham suspended on both four elliptic and four C-springs. Dark green lower body. Black moldings, upper body and boot. Moldings striped light green. Dark green carriage with a broad black stripe and two fine stripes of light green. Green morocco trimmings for the lower back, lower and upper quarters, and cushion top. Green cloth trimmings for upper back, doors, head lining and driver's seat. Wheels 38″ and 45″. Body 52″ wide. *The Hub*, vol. 27, Nov. 1885, pl. 63.

122. BARKER BROUGHAM. Curving lines and a door clos-
ing above the bottom line mark this model, the original design coming from the famous London shops of Barker &
Co. Wheels 34″ and 43″. *The Hub,* vol. 32, Oct. 1890, pl. 51.

123. EXTENSION-FRONT BROUGHAM. Although this model appears sufficiently extended to be called either a coupé or a clarence, in the United States it was frequently called an extension-front brougham. It was often used as a family carriage. The number on the lamp of this one seems to indicate that it was a public cab. (Photo from Smithsonian Institution.)

124. COUPE. In America, the term "coupé" and "brougham" were frequently synonomous during the middle of the 19th century. The mock top-joint was nonfunctional and was for ornamentation only. Wheels 45½″ and 49½″. *The Coachmaker's Magazine*, vol. 3, July 1857, pl. 25.

125. COUPE. The editors here apply the term "coupé" to what might have been called an extension-front brougham, with a hinged child's seat in the extension. Deep crimson lake body with a fine carmine stripe. Black upper panel. Deep crimson lake carriage striped with black, edged with two fine stripes of carmine. Brown satin trimming. Gold mountings. Wheels 40″ and 48″. *The New York Coach-maker's Magazine*, vol. 12, Jan. 1871, pl. 31.

126. COUPE. Another variety had an octagon front to accommodate the folding child's seat. Black upper panels. Black moldings with a fine stripe of yellow on the edges. Green lower panels. Dark green carriage with a yellow stripe. Green cloth trimming. Wheels 34″ and 42″. Body 48″ wide. *The Hub*, vol. 29, Nov. 1887, pl. 63.

127. CABRIOLET. Acquiring four wheels and a driving seat early in the 19th century, the cabriolet became a highly popular vehicle in both Europe and the United States. This style was also known as a panel-boot Victoria. Amber brown panels. London-smoke pillars. Black moldings with a fine carmine stripe. Carmine carriage striped black. Brown cloth trimming. *The Hub*, vol. 36, Aug. 1894, p. 340.

128. CABRIOLET. The cabriolet name was also applied to a sort of double phaeton, like this example, which was a popular upper-middle-class family carriage. The high wheelhouse and the absence of a perch enabled easy turning in a narrow street. Wheels 38″ and 50″. *The New York Coach-maker's Magazine*, vol. 9, Dec. 1867, pl. 26.

129. CABRIOLET. The carriage, with appropriately dressed
coachman, stands in front of a carriage house. (Photo from Smithsonian Institution.)

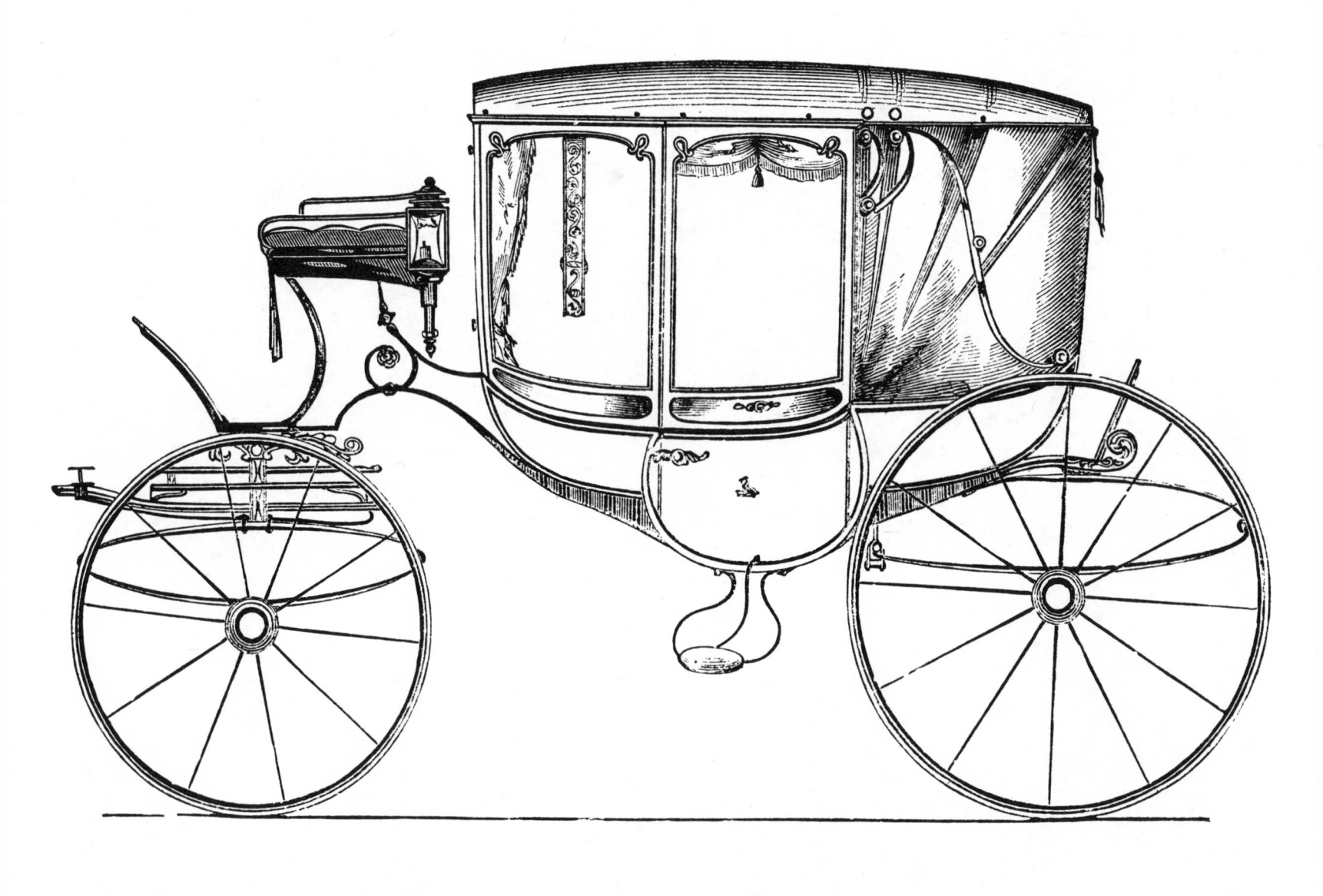

130. CALECHE. The caleche had limited use because of its high expense. Though versatile, it required a practical mechanic to remove the front and most of the top. When altered they became pleasant half-top vehicles. They cost from $800 to $1000 in 1862. Wheels 41″ and 48″. *The Coach-maker's Magazine*, vol. 2, Oct. 1856, pl. 23, fig. 51.

131. CALECHE. This is another style, fitted only with the half-top. During the first half of the 19th century this carriage would have been called a barouche. It cost $600 to $750 in 1862. Wheels 42″ and 50″. Catalog of Lawrence, Bradley and Pardee, New Haven, Conn., 1862.

132. MOUNTAIN WAGON. A heavy variety of spring wagon, the mountain wagon, as the name implies, was commonly used in rugged mountainous country, especially in the west, during the late 19th century. They were therefore often provided with a brake. Dark green body. Red or yellow carriage. Black leather trimming. Wheels 42″ and 48″. Catalog of the Studebaker Bros. Mfg. Co., South Bend, Ind., Dec. 1903, p. 107.

133. MOUNTAIN WAGON. Equipped with three or four seats and a luggage rack, the mountain wagon could serve as a depot wagon, carry excursion parties, or be put to use in regular stage service. Dark green body. Red or yellow carriage. Black leather trimming. Wheels 42″ and 48″. Catalog of the Studebaker Bros. Mfg. Co., South Bend, Ind., Dec. 1903, p. 107.

134. OPERA BUS. Also known as a private omnibus, the opera bus began to develop in about 1870. It was used as a family vehicle and, with the roof rail, served to some degree as a depot wagon. Those provided with a roof seat, such as this example, were convenient for viewing horse racing or other sporting events. Dark green main body and door panels. Coaching-red seat risers, footboard, boot rockers and lattice work. Remainder of body black. Coaching-red carriage striped black. Outside seat trimmed with leather. Inside trimmings of green or light-colored cloth. Wheels 36″ and 46″. Width across top 58″. *The Hub*, vol. 43, Apr. 1901, pl. 503.

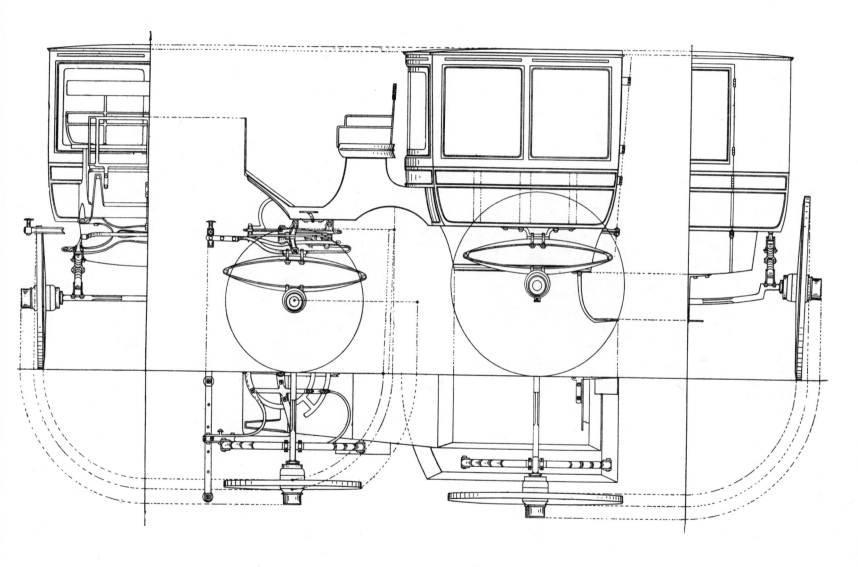

135. PRIVATE OMNIBUS. This model could be constructed with a top that was removable at the belt rail. When converted, the vehicle became a comfortable open wagonette.

These carriages were popular among well-to-do families living in suburban areas. Wheels 36″ and 46″. *The Hub*, vol. 51, July 1909, p. 124.

136. VICTORIA. Named in honor of the English queen, the victoria developed over a period of years in England and on the Continent. It began to gain prominence in the United States after 1870. The victoria was essentially a phaeton with a driving seat supported above the dash by a skeleton framework, and was commonly used by the upper classes for park driving. Body with dark green panels with black moldings. Dark green carriage with black or yellow striping. Dark green morocco and cloth trimmings. Wheels 32″ and 41″. Track 46″ in front and 56″ in rear. Body 48″ at arm pillar. *The Hub,* vol. 29, Nov. 1887, color plate XCI.

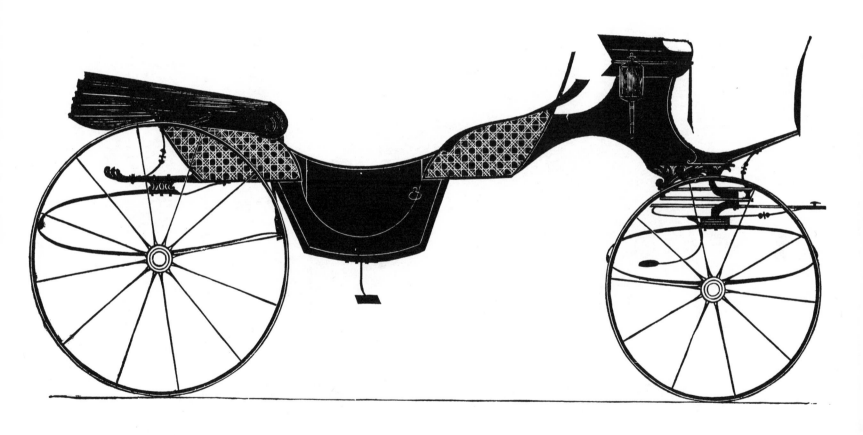

137. VIS-A-VIS. Pleasant summer carriages of this type originated during the 18th century, and were known as sociables. By the mid-19th century the term "vis-à-vis" (face-to-face) was coming into general use for the vehicle. Wheels 38″ and 46″. *The New York Coach-maker's Magazine*, vol. 6, July 1864, pl. 5.

138. VIS-A-VIS. With a standing top protecting driver as well as passengers, this model is somewhat suggestive of an extension-front rockaway. The rolled-up curtain visible at the top could enclose the carriage in foul weather. Folded on the floor of the front portion is a rain apron that could be pulled up to protect the driver and his companion. Dark green main panels. Front part and seats black. Dark green carriage with two fine stripes of light green. Green morocco trimming for seats and backs; green cloth for the doors and head lining. Wheels 39″ and 45″. Track 56″. *The Hub*, vol. 28, June 1886, pl. 22.

139. WAGONETTE. The carriage originated in England during the 1840s. Its principal features were longitudinal rear seats and a rear entrance. Built in a wide variety of sizes and styles, some were useful as family carriages while others served as public vehicles—either as excursion vehicles or as a sort of summer omnibus. Brewster and Baldwin, of New York City, built this unusual family version with an extra, forward-facing seat. Wheels 42″ and 48″. *The New York Coach-maker's Magazine*, vol. 10, June 1868, pl. 1 (bottom).

140. EIGHT-PASSENGER WAGONETTE. Made open or with standing top, this typical example was large enough to serve as either a public or a family carriage. Large rear panel dark green. Other parts of body black. Dark green carriage with two stripes of carmine. Green morocco trimmings. Wheels 35″ and 46″. Track 50″ in front and 56″ in rear. Body 44″ wide at top of front seat. *The Hub,* vol. 26, Dec. 1884, pl. 70.

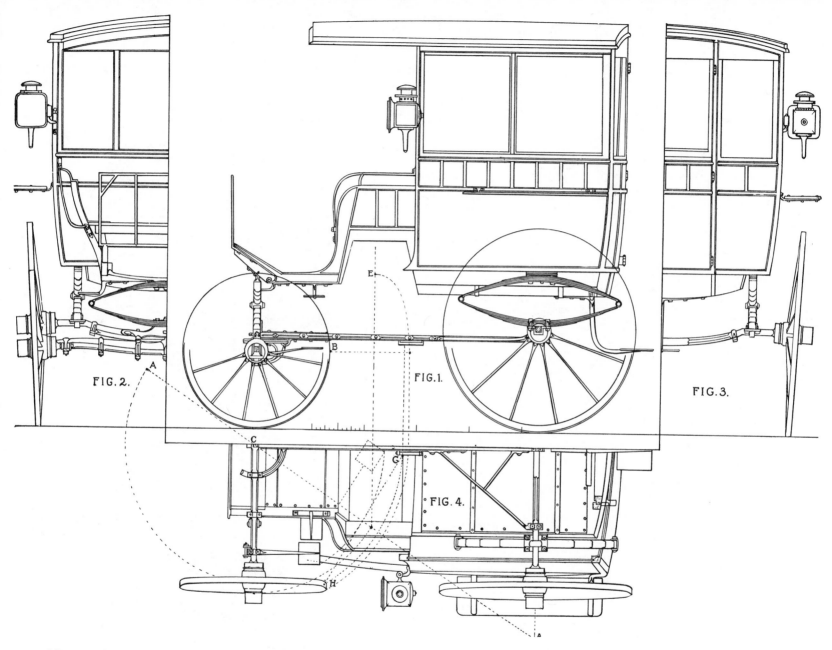

FIG. 2.   FIG.1.   FIG.3.

FIG. 4.

141. WAGONETTE. A family vehicle with glasses in the sides and door, and accommodating 8 passengers, this model has been made to appear shorter than the preceding model by shortening the sides and swelling the rear end. Amber brown seat, belt panels, stanhope pillars, and brackets. Main lower panels and all remaining body parts black. Moldings striped with a fine stripe or light amber. Dark amber carriage striped black. Light Bedford cord trimming. *The Hub*, vol. 42, June 1900, p. 114.

142. BREAK. This is a break in its original and true sense. It was used for breaking and exercising horses, eliminating the danger of damage to a fine carriage. Painted Indian red. All irons, except axles and springs, black. Green cloth seat cushion. Silver mountings. Wheels 39″ and 57″. *The Carriage Monthly*, vol. 26, Sept. 1890, pl. 45.

143. ROAD-COACH. While road-coaches were frequently public vehicles, they were also used by wealthy families as private carriages. The John Wanamaker family took several European tours in theirs during the 1890s. This photo was taken at Versailles in 1894. (Photo from Smithsonian Institution.)

144. DRAG. The drag was a lighter version of the public road-coach, but was intended for recreational and sporting purposes. They were popular for picnicking, and offered convenient grandstand seats at the race tracks. Obviously, they were vehicles for the wealthy. Wheels 41″ and 48″. *The New York Coach-maker's Magazine,* vol. 3, Jan. 1861, pl. 26.

145. DRAG. This typical drag, by Hincks and Johnson, Bridgeport, Conn., contained ample space in the front and rear boots and in the imperial on the roof for the storage of equipment, food and drink. The imperial opened into a lunch table, and the door to the rear boot was hinged at the bottom, to provide a serving table when let down. Included in the equipment was an iron ladder to assist ladies in mounting the roof seats. Servants rode inside. Lower panels of body bottle green. Coaching-red upper panels, rockers, seat risers and toe-board. Coaching-red carriage, with ¾″ black stripes. Drab cloth trimming inside; amber-colored French pigskin outside. Wheels 40″ and 50″. *The Carriage Monthly*, vol. 15, Oct. 1879, pl. 50.

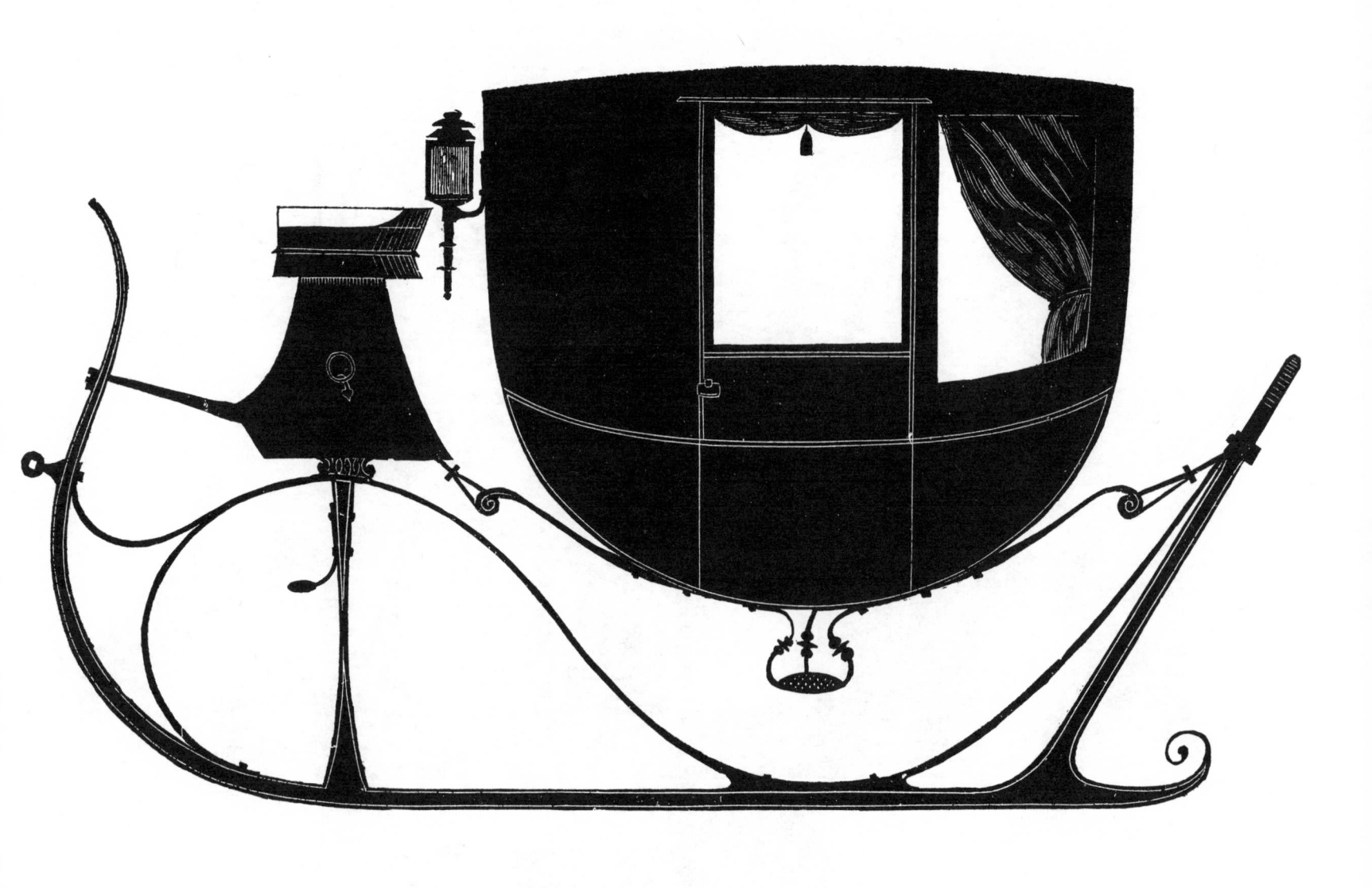

146. BOOBY-HUT. An enclosed carriage body suspended by leather braces on sleigh runners was known as a booby-hut or as a Boston booby, indicating its place of origin as well as the area where it enjoyed greatest use. The bodies were often made expressly for use on runners. Body 6′ long. *The New York Coach-maker's Magazine*, vol. 7, Sept. 1865, pl. 13.

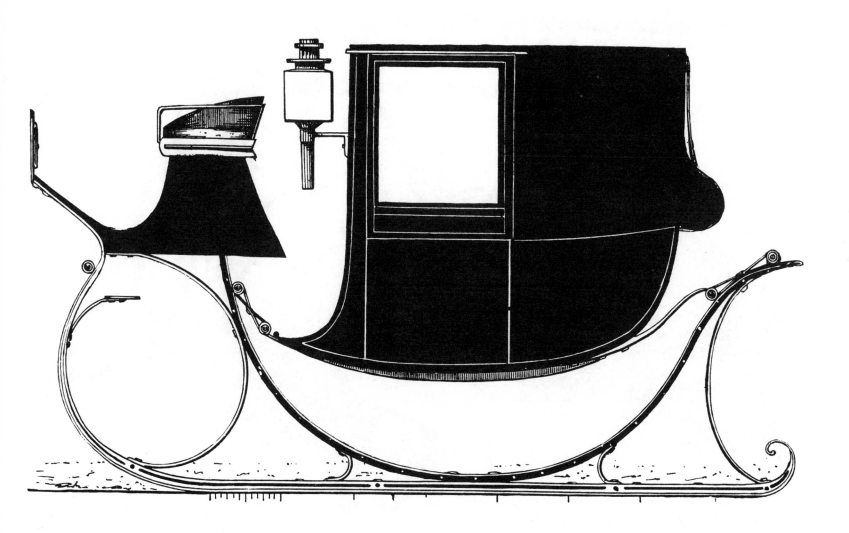

147. BOOBY-HUT. The coupé body was also popular for use in booby-huts. This one has a relic of earlier days—the sword case—on the rear of the body. This receptacle was ac-cessible from the inside of the carriage, and was originally used to contain a weapon to be used in the event of an encounter with highwaymen. *The Hub,* vol. 24, July 1882, p. 219.

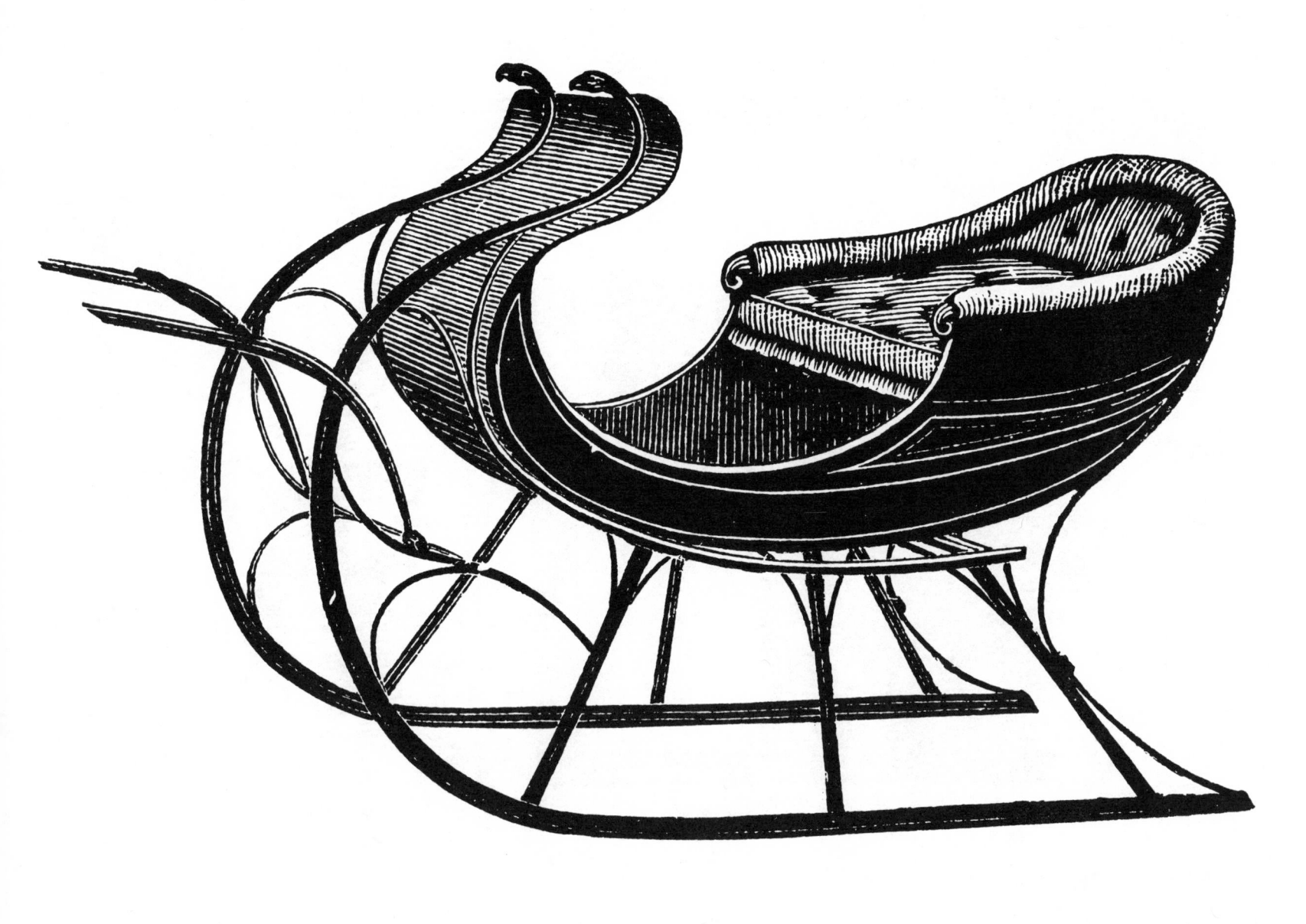

148. ALBANY CUTTER. This plate, drawn from ambrotypes furnished by the James Goold firm in Albany, N.Y., shows the ever-popular Albany cutter, also known as a swell-body or Goold cutter. Though originated by Goold nearly a quarter of a century earlier, this sleigh was also built by hundreds of other builders until the end of the carriage era. *The New York Coach-maker's Magazine*, vol. 1, Nov. 1858, pl. 21.

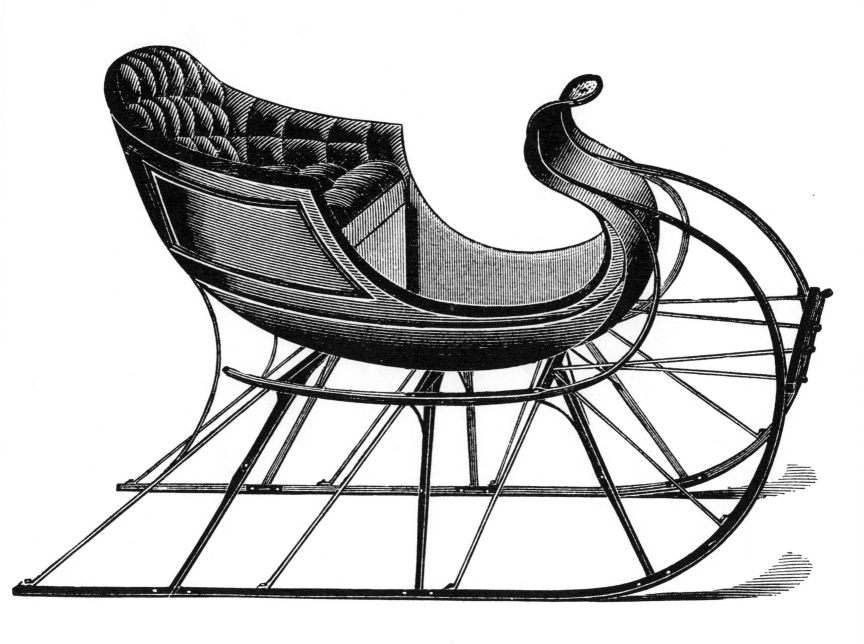

149. ALBANY CUTTER. This attractive model, built by The Northwestern Cutter Works, of Ft. Atkinson, Wisc., was 6 feet long. Dark green body with a light green seat panel and fine gold-and-white striping. Dark lake runners striped straw color. Green cloth or plush trimming. Many cutters were ornately decorated with brightly colored scrollwork, or heraldic devices. *The Carriage Monthly*, vol. 16, Aug. 1880, pl. 36.

150. PORTLAND CUTTER. Probably the most popular of all sleighs was the Portland (or Kimball) cutter, developed in the mid-19th century by Peter Kimball and his sons, of Portland, Me. Whereas the Albany cutter had an outline sweeping in a continuous curve, the Portland cutter had a "corner" at the bottom. The ornate example shown here, built by Kimball & Clement, of Portland, was trimmed with silk plush, had silver mountings and cost $150. The S-curve of the back panel makes this an ogee Portland. *The New York Coach-maker's Magazine*, vol. 2, Sept. 1859, pl. 11.

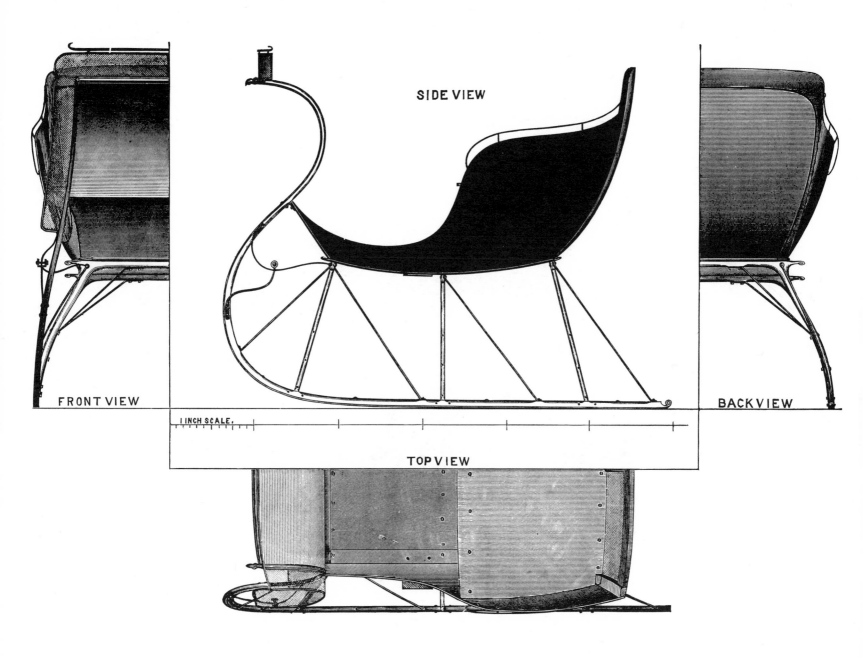

SIDE VIEW

FRONT VIEW

BACK VIEW

1 INCH SCALE.

TOP VIEW

151. PORTLAND CUTTER. The standard Portland design is shown here. By 1910 cutters of this type could be purchased for $20. Lake body panels. Black moldings with a fine stripe of yellow or gold. Other parts of the body black. Lake carriage striped with black and gold. Brown cloth trimmings. Length 5'5". *The Carriage Monthly*, vol. 23, Aug. 1887, p. 125.

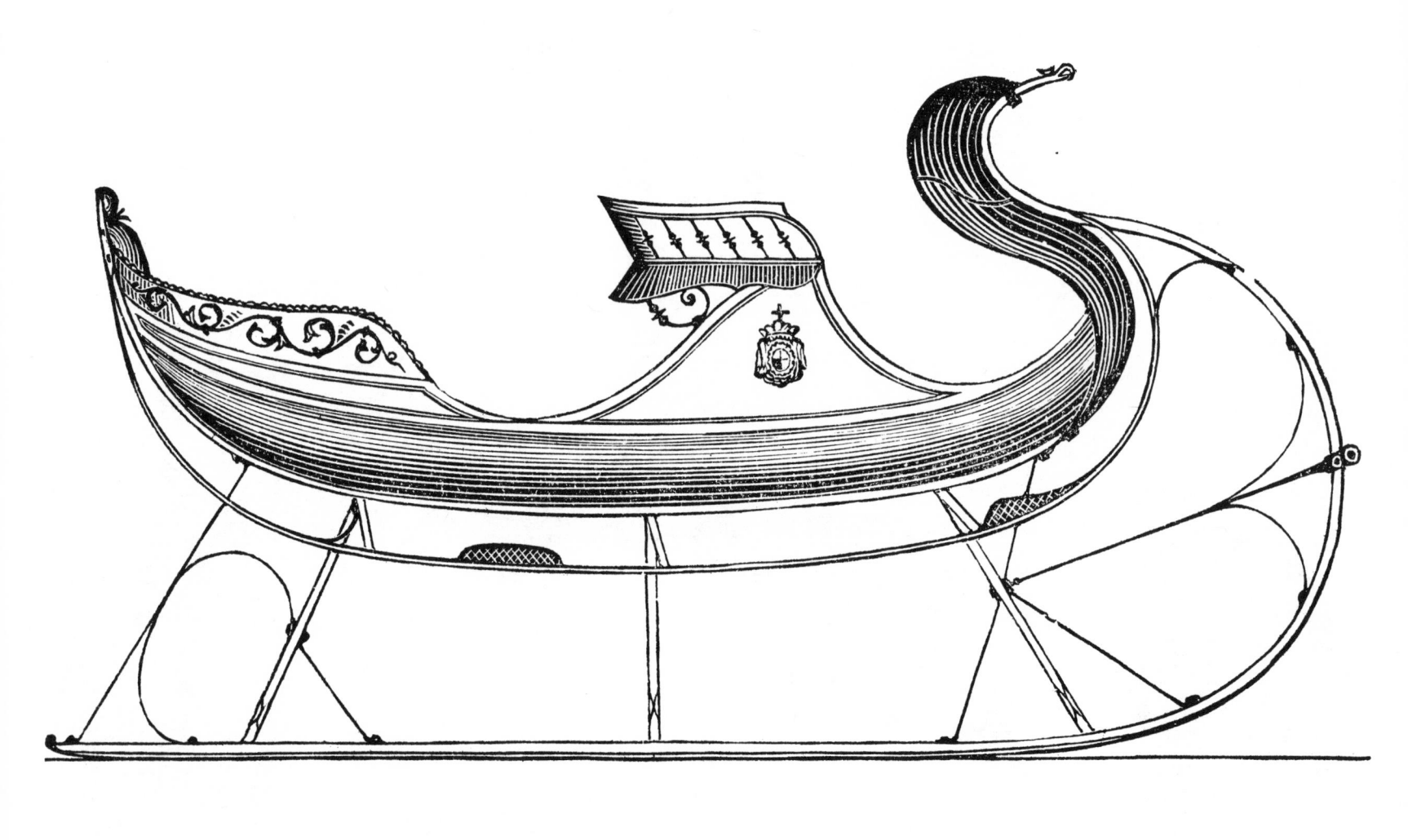

152. SLEIGH. Sleighs were often brightly finished, with panels elaborately decorated with scrollwork and other varying designs, as shown on this swell-side four-passenger sleigh.

Body 63″ long. *The Coach-maker's Magazine*, vol. 3, Sept. 1857, pl. 31, fig. 2.

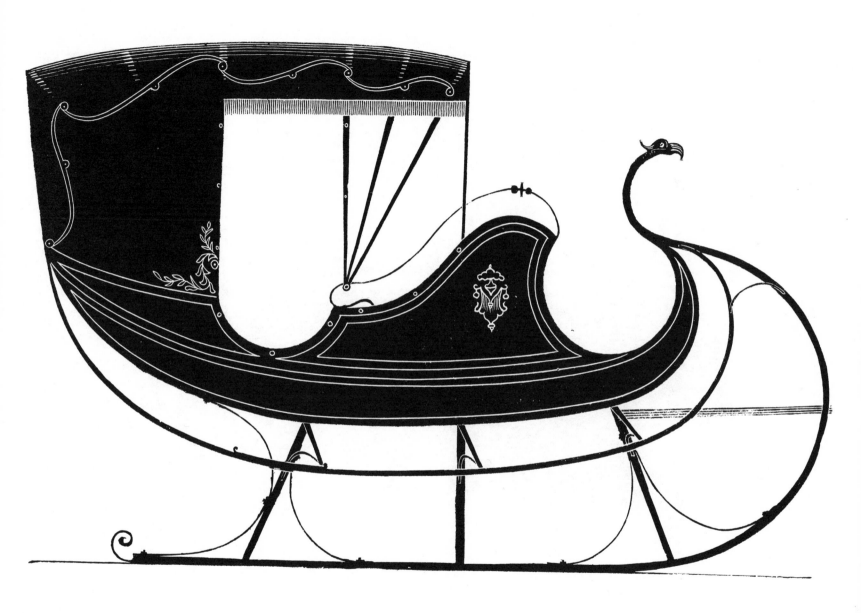

153. SLEIGH. While most sleighs were open, a few were equipped with falling tops, such as this six-passenger, extension-top sleigh. Plush trimmings. Body 8′9″ long. Track 40″.

The New York Coach-maker's Magazine, vol. 3, Sept. 1860, pl. 12.

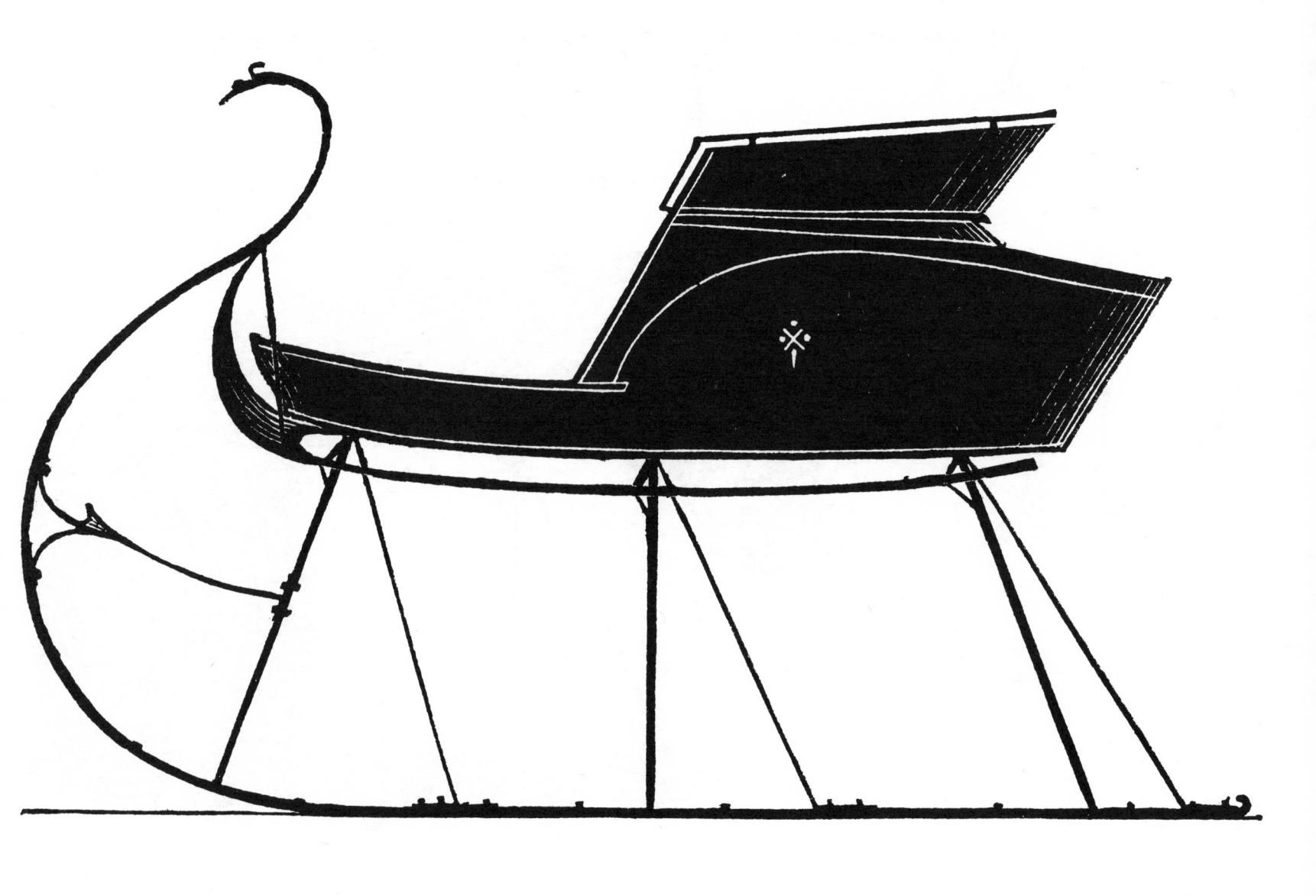

154. COAL-BOX SLEIGH. A popular buggy design was borrowed for this model, which cost $100. Body 45″ long and 27″ wide. *The New York Coach-maker's Magazine*, vol. 8, Oct. 1866, pl. 19 (bottom).

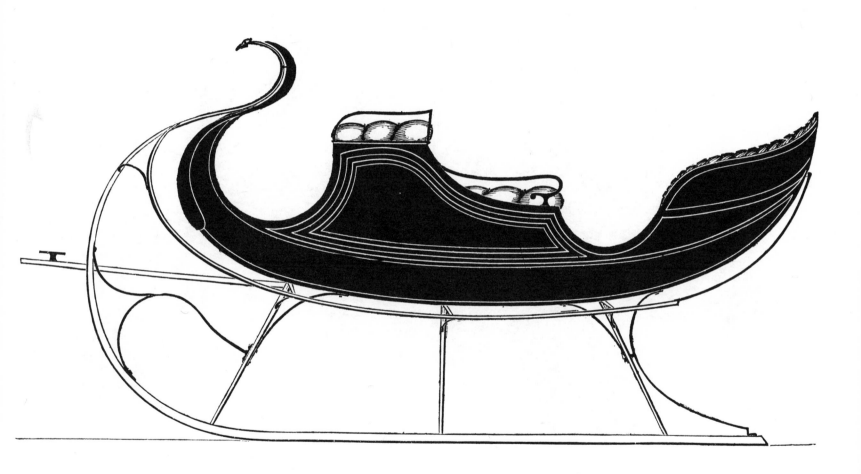

155. SLEIGH. This attractive six-passenger family model was built by Curtis, Bowen & Co. of Kingston, New York. Lake body. Vermilion running part. Body 9'5" long. Track 40". *The New York Coach-maker's Magazine,* vol. 10, Aug. 1868, pl. 11.

156. PONY SLEIGH. This ladies' vehicle had a rumble for one or two servants which was often supported by iron stays to give the sleigh a lighter appearance. Bright lake body with black and gold stripes. Black moldings and area under main seat. Light carmine running part striped black and edged with gold. Red plush trimming. Bright lake carpet with black figures. *The Hub*, vol. 25, Oct. 1883, pl. 69.

157. CABRIOLET SLEIGH. This high-fashion model borrows a carriage design of a cabriolet body (sometimes called a panel-boot Victoria). The driving cushion is not often seen on less elaborate sleighs. The wire snow screens on the top and sides of the dash, which prevented snow from being thrown into the sleigh by the horses' hooves, and the ornamental plumes, are other evidences of quality. Ultramarine body with broad cream-colored stripe on panels, an inch from the moldings. Moldings black with fine cane-colored stripe. Black dickey (or driving) seat. Blue dash striped like body. Light blue running part striped cream. Blue plush trimming. Blue figured carpet. White horsehair plumes. Silver mountings. *The Hub*, vol. 24, July 1882, pl. 44.

158. HUDSON RIVER SLEIGH. *The Hub* unfortunately did not list the price of this elaborate six-passenger, shell-body model. The crane-neck, so useful to carriages (front wheels could cut under it), serves no functional purpose here; it relieves the front of the sleigh of an otherwise heavy appearance. Medium green shellwork striped gold and carmine. Carmine running part with a narrow black stripe and two fine stripes of gold. Green cloth trimming. Dark green carpet. Silver mountings. Body 9'7" long, 39" wide. *The Hub*, vol. 27, Aug. 1885, pl. 41.

159. SLEIGH. Although sleighs did not generally feature springs, this one is hung on side springs. The body is of the Portland type. Dark green body striped red. Carmine running part striped black. *The Carriage Monthly*, vol. 48, Apr. 1912, pl. 1481.

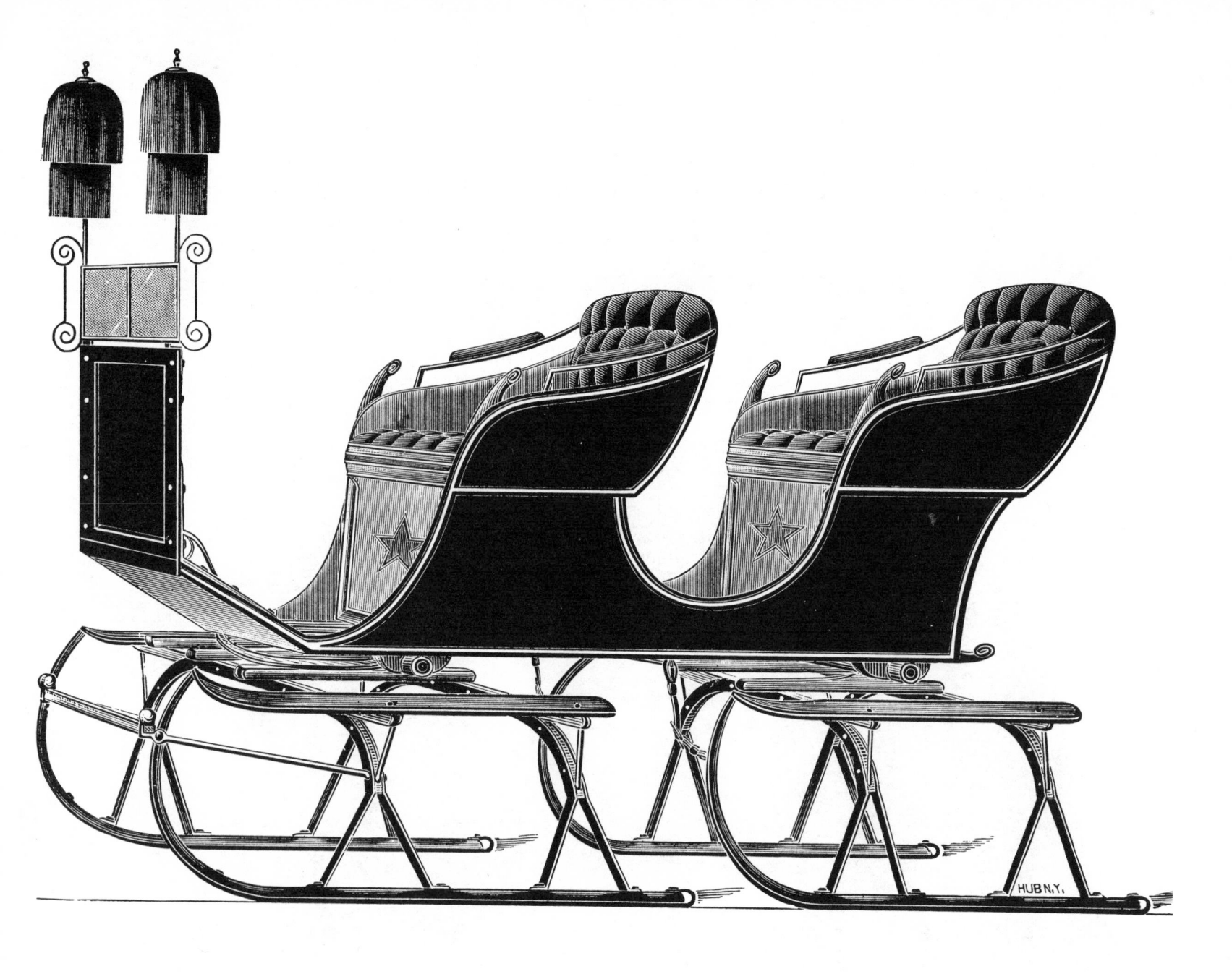

160. BOB SLEIGH. Unlike the cutter on continuous runners, larger sleighs were often placed on bob-runners, or two short sleds. The oscillating motion of these two provided a smoother ride over uneven and rutted roads. Black body with green seat panels and a fine straw-color stripe on the moldings. Maroon carriage with two stripes of carmine. Maroon cloth trimming. Green, brown and red plumes. *The Hub,* vol. 29, Aug. 1887, pl. 38.

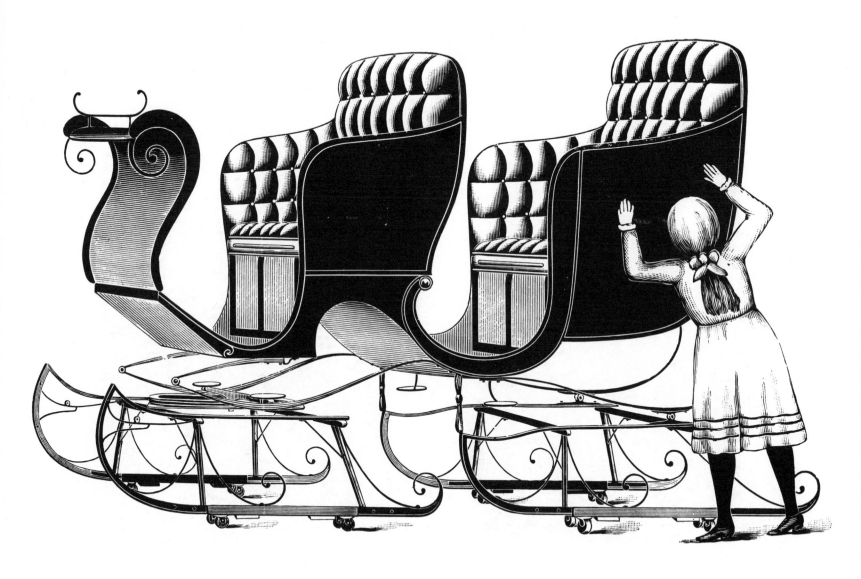

161. BOB SLEIGH. Some bob-runner sleighs were suspended on steel springs. This one is resting on rollers which were helpful in moving the sleigh about on a stable or carriage-house floor. Dark green body with black moldings, striped with carmine. Carmine carriage with two black stripes. Green cloth trimming. Catalog of F. O. Bailey Carriage Co., Portland, Me., c. 1894.

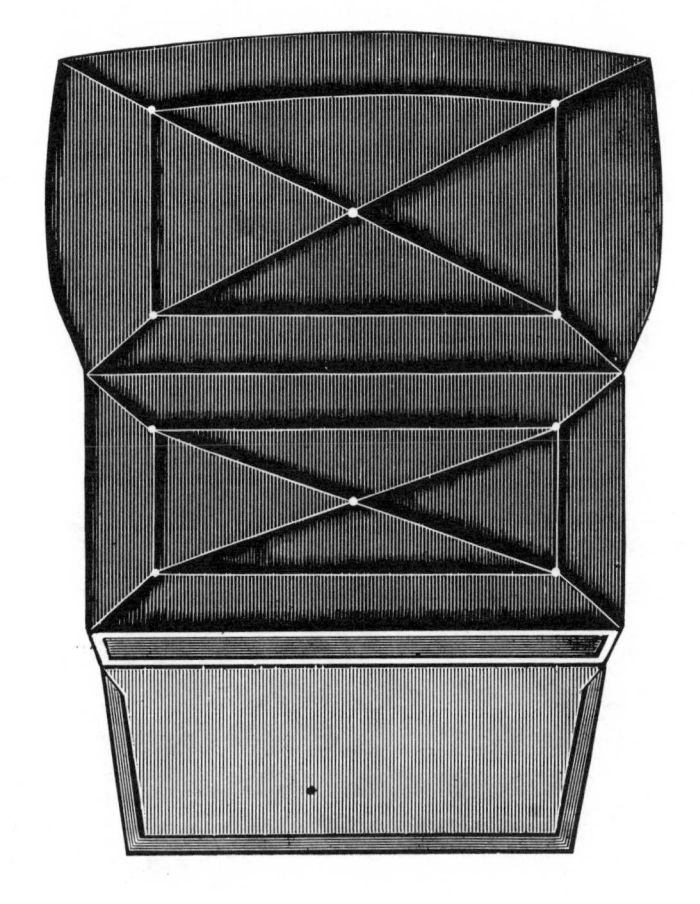 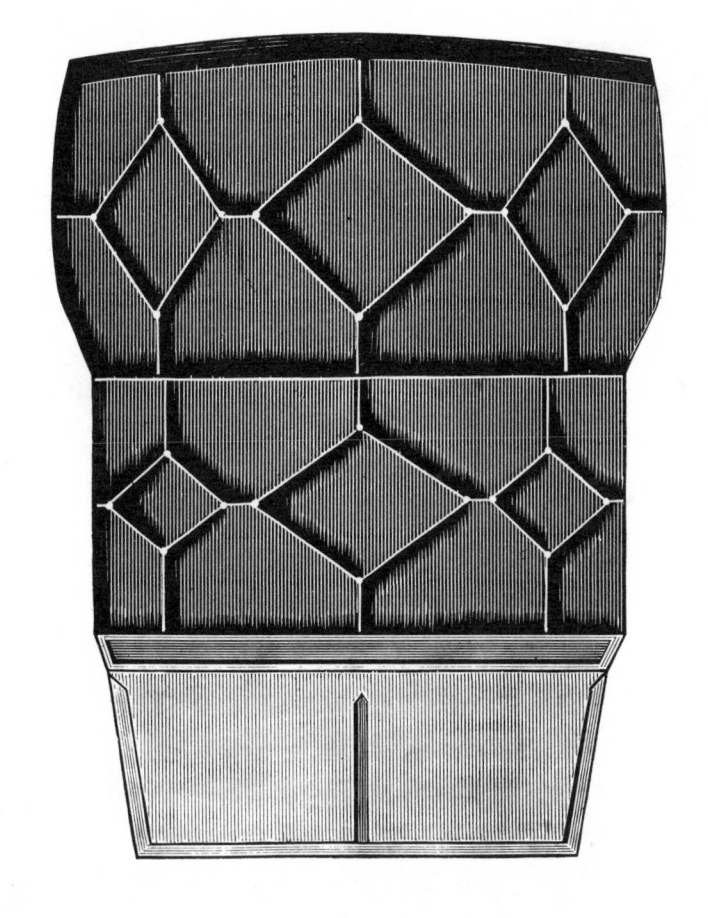

162. These two illustrations show patterns for trimming light and medium work such as a buggy, surrey or phaeton. The back, cushion and fall (ornamental flap hanging under the front edge of cushion) are shown. The tufting buttons were not drawn down tightly to avoid deep crevices in which moths could hide. Precaution against moths was also the reason for the relatively plain design. *The Hub*, vol. 25, May 1883, p. 95.

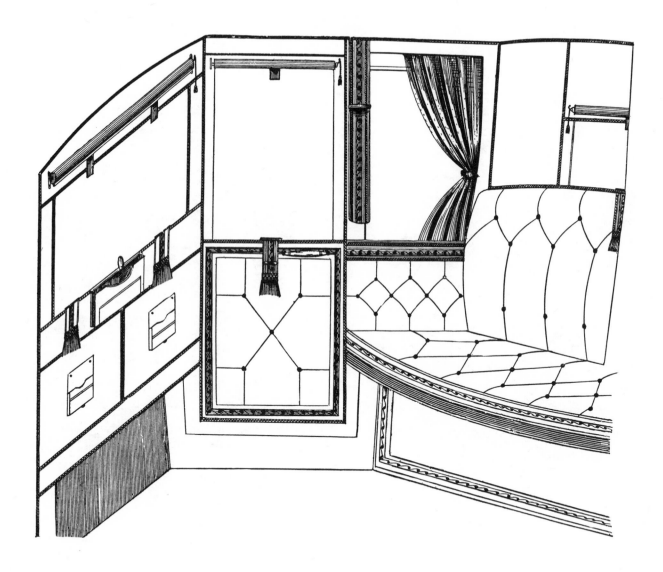

163. Here is a pattern for a coupé rockaway. The cushion is faced with broad lace. The mirror and card cases in front and the door pulls are covered with morocco. *The Hub,* vol. 25, June 1883, p. 160.

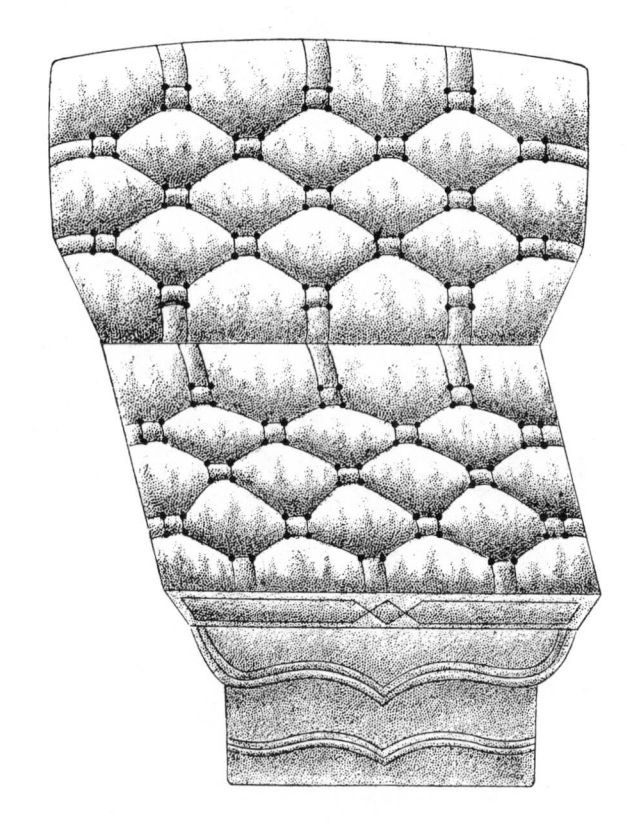
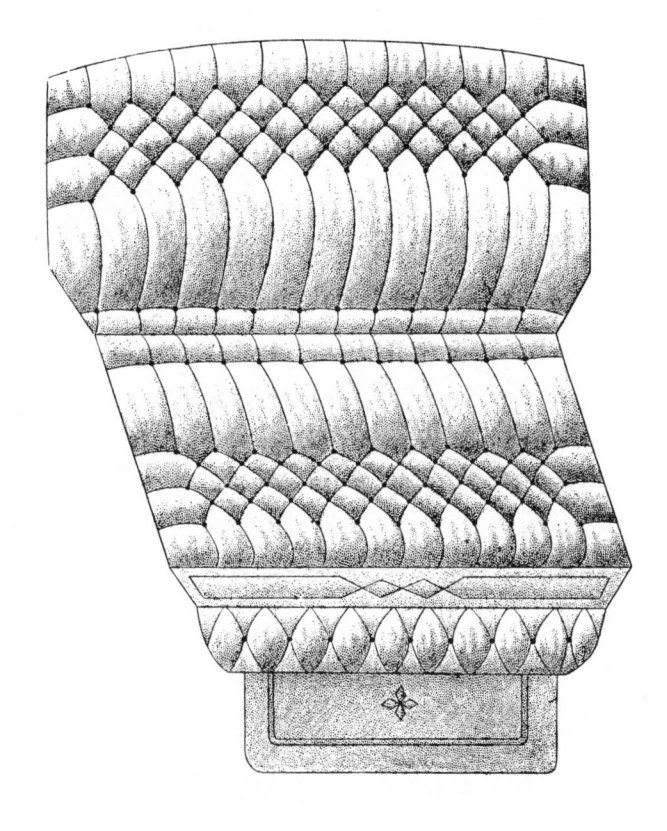

164. Two more patterns for light and medium work are these from the Youngstown Carriage and Wagon Co. The tufted section of the fall in the second design was sewn in on a sewing machine, with only light wadding. *The Hub*, vol. 33, Sept. 1891, p. 297.

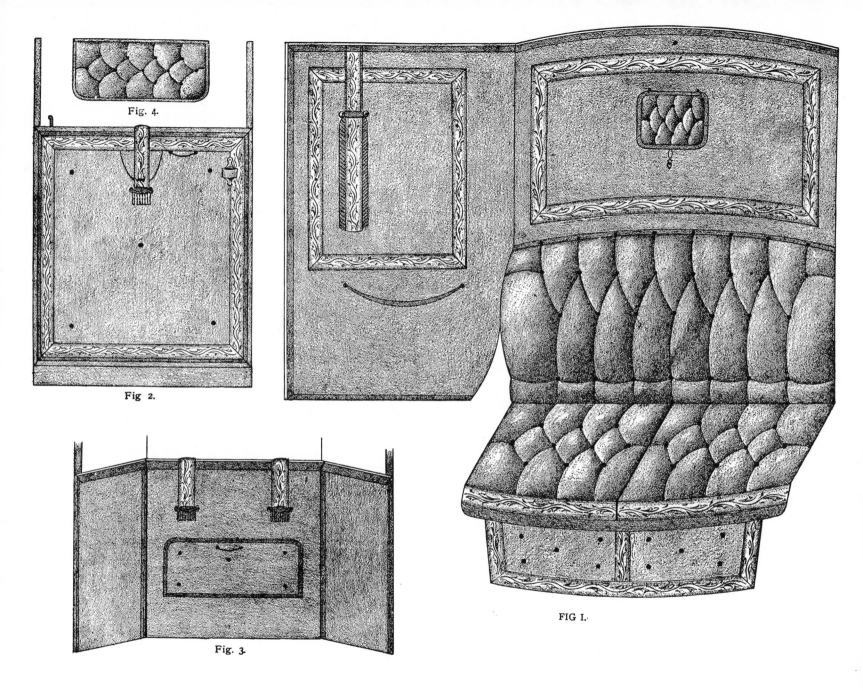

Fig. 4.

Fig 2.

Fig. 3.

FIG I.

165. This trimming pattern for a coupé is also suitable for a brougham, with the front accordingly modified. Fig. 4, shown above the door, is the child's seat, which is also shown in the folded position in the front view, fig. 3. *The Hub*, vol. 29, Feb. 1888, pp. 784–5.

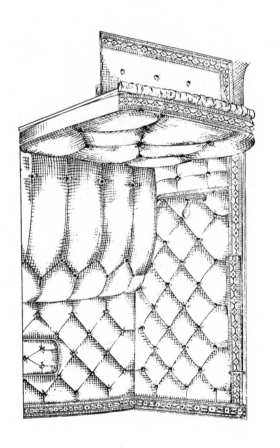

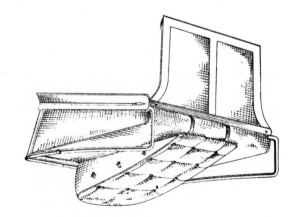

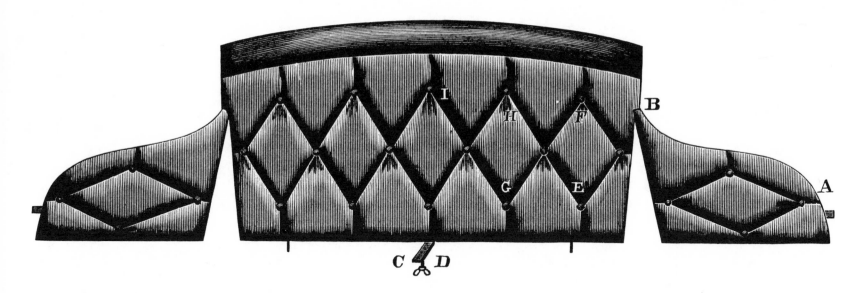

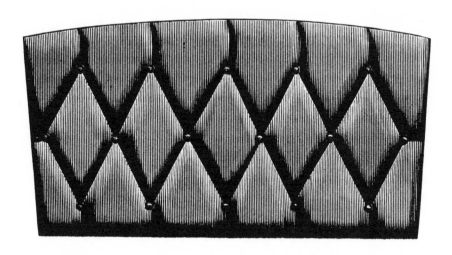

167. An appropriate pattern for a Portland cutter shows the back, with ends, and the cushion. The end panels were omitted in some sleighs, giving them a rather unfinished appearance. *The Carriage Monthly*, vol. 23, Dec. 1887, p. 244.